Sacred Self

EVERYDAY RITUALS FOR THE MODERN WOMAN

NICOLETTE HALLADAY   TARA HAISLIP

APRIL AZZOLINO   KRISTEN TOSCANO

ROXY RAPEDIUS   JANNA LEMUR

RACHEL CAREY-MCELWANEY

ABIGAIL MENSAH-BONSU   SWATI KAMESWAR

REGYNA CURTIS   LEISA QUAGLIATA

MELINDA NAKAGAWA, M.SC,   ALLIE THEISS

CHARLOTTE DE JAEGHER   VANDANA SINHA

HEATHER LIVESAY BROWN   RUTH FAE

ISBN #979-8-9909217-8-8

Your Sacred Invitation

Dear Reader,

I invite you to unlock the transformative power with the rituals laid out in this book. Sacred Self: Everyday Rituals for the Modern Woman is a heartfelt guide filled with practical wisdom and impactful practices from experts in self-care, healing, and spirituality. Whether you're new to self-care or looking to deepen your spiritual practice, this book is a beautiful companion to creating a sacred space in your daily life.

Within these pages, you'll discover a variety of rituals designed to support every aspect of your journey—from creating sacred spaces and embracing your authentic voice, to healing from heartbreak and connecting with your deepest truths. Dive into daily rituals, holistic healing practices, and ancestral wisdom. Learn how to stay mindful, harness the power of the new moon, and unlock your unlimited potential.

In Sacred Self, you'll also find personal stories from the authors themselves, sharing how these practices have transformed their lives. These stories offer insight and inspiration, illustrating how these rituals can bring positive changes to your life too.

Get comfortable, grab a pen and something to write with, and immerse yourself in these beautiful rituals. Let the authors guide you through these practices as you experience the incredible magic within each one, or explore the practices that resonate most with you.

Share this book with the women in your life and let's make advocating for our sacred self a normal and accessible practice for all women. Open this book and begin your journey to a more meaningful, enriched, and sacred life.

Enjoy!

- Sacred Self Authors

Create Space

THIS PRACTICE IS to help you step back from things in your life that may be overwhelming you. There is so much great information about self-care out there in the market, but it's very easy to feel completely overwhelmed by the options, especially if you're in an energetically chaotic place.

As you go through this book, you're going to read many amazing self-care rituals and lean into the one that speaks to you the loudest. If you're having trouble hearing which one has the strongest pull on your attention, come back to this chapter to help you find some space.

This practice is simply about turning down the volume on your thoughts so you can hear your intuition answer the question: *What do I need, right now?*

Materials/Supplies Needed:

All optional

• Blanket

• Tea

- Journal

- Favorite spot to sit in your house

- Favorite spot to sit outside

Time Needed to Complete the Ritual:

The time needed is based on your internal clock; it is complete when you feel relaxed. This could be anywhere from 30 seconds to 10 minutes, or more.

Optimal Time of Day to Perform Ritual:

The best time to practice this ritual is when it is most quiet in your day. I recommend either early morning or late evening. I do *not* recommend trying to do this in the middle of your day; doing so will only add to your stress.

Description of Ritual

[1] I invite you to:

1. Find a quiet space that is your favorite place to be—in your home or outdoors.
2. Get settled—in a seated position, lying down, in a chair, sitting on the floor or ground.
3. Close your eyes.
4. Take three deep inhales and exhales. Then place your hands over your heart and listen to your regular breathing pattern.

---

1. If you find yourself overthinking this practice, you can simplify the process. Think about when the quietest time in your day occurs. Make that your time to just be, however that looks for you.

If you're feeling extremely overwhelmed, you don't have to do a meditation, journal, or craft activity. Sometimes just sitting and being present in your space and body is all you need to help you listen to your intuition for what you need next—relaxation, meditation, sitting outside, and so on.

Find that time. Find that space. Sit there as often as you feel called to do so.

5. As you ease into your regular breathing pattern, allow the sound of your breathing to be replaced with the sounds around you.
6. If a thought enters your mind, let it pass you by like the cars on a highway—acknowledge its existence but let it go.
7. Ask yourself: *What is it I need right now?*
8. In the peace of the space you're physically in, sit with this question until you find a sense of peaceful space within your mind and heart.
9. When you feel ready to come back to your physical body and the room, slowly open your eyes, move your hands and feet, and sit with what came through for you.
10. Whatever action you feel called to next—do it. There is no right or wrong way to self-care.

For further guidance on this, I invite you to listen to my guided meditation that will walk you through the above:

https://www.groundedenergy111.com/book-sacred-self

Follow the QR code to Create a Space Guided Meditation

THE EVOLUTION OF SPACE

When trying to find a sense of peace with my life and my corporate career, I used to be on social media regularly. I lived the cycle of:

Happy Monday!

Taco Tuesday!

Hump Day!

Mini-Friday!

Fri-Yay!

Trying to find a way to look forward to each day, and constantly wishing for the weekend, I remember thinking, *Is this really what my life has been reduced to?* I kept wondering when my life had been reduced to this routine. The more I reflected, the more I began to notice the attitudes of the people around me. I had surrounded myself with others in corporate on the same grind, both physically and through social media.

It started to make me feel uneasy about my career direction. In response, I searched for ways to work on changing my mindset. Initially, it was simply to have a more positive outlook on my life, but this soon began to snowball into the question: *Is this what I want for my life?*

This question concerned me because I had worked so hard to get to where I was; the thought of completely changing direction felt unsettling. What scared me the most was that it hit the nerve about how I viewed a healthy work-life balance. My beliefs about money, work, education, and how I want to live my life went against the societal norm; they still do.

So, instead of exploring this question, I tried to run away from it, and spent years down the rabbit hole of self-care overload. I think, in our own ways, we can all do this. I started a daily routine that heavily focused on food, exercise, journaling, meditation, and yoga. It did not take long before it felt like I was trying to put a Band-Aid on a lacerated artery. The self-care routine wasn't making me feel any better about my career-life balance, although it was bringing more realization to the situation. The realization was what I needed while, at the same time, it felt extremely frustrating.

I had hit the proverbial wall and decided to sit down to answer the question about what I really wanted from my life. The honest answer was that I did not believe in my corporate career path. I didn't feel like I was living for *my* dreams but that I was living for *someone else's* dream.

I found myself daydreaming about running my own business as a solo entrepreneur. As I started to change who I surrounded myself with, my life filled up with entrepreneurial women. I loved listening to how they didn't have to answer to anyone but themselves and their clients, that there was no cap on how much they could make, and that they had time-freedom.

It was in this moment I ditched the overzealous self-care routine to figure *me* out.

I didn't come back to a set self-care routine until after the birth of my first child. This time, I didn't listen to any of the media's advice around this but simply looked at my life in the present moment to take note of what I needed. It was space. As a first-time mom, I didn't know how much space I needed, but I recognized it was space.

I developed a simple routine around my baby's routine, which was easy since his sleep schedule was like clockwork. My self-care routine changed frequently during those first two years of his life before it settled on a simple routine of waking at 4am to have my cup of coffee and sit in the silence of the house, reading or writing until he woke up.

This routine went on for a couple of years until I became pregnant with my second child.

THE UPSIDE DOWN

My second son decided to join us during a time of complete turmoil. We were living with my in-laws and I had lost my job. Trying to re-establish a self-care routine was very difficult and I found myself simply taking things day-by-day until things untangled themselves.

It was hard to get into a flow of *allowing* things to unfold while living with a lot of stress and the expectations of other people. I became too overwhelmed trying to think about *tomorrow*. My self-care during this time was to simply focus on *today*.

Only focusing on *today* continued for a solid year before things started to untangle themselves.

One month after the year mark of my life knotting up, an opportunity landed in my lap. Soon after, an opportunity landed in my husband's lap. Then within two months of those opportunities, we were back to being financially solvent, moved out of my in-laws, and relocated halfway across the country.

I knew something like this was possible. It's happened many times, in smaller ways, throughout my spiritual journey. The hardest part was riding the wave of the total chaos we were in to allow it to unfold.

Once we were on the other side of the chaos, I was faced with a whole new version of myself and the space to develop a new self-care routine that helped me think about *tomorrow*, not just *today*.

As of the writing of this chapter, I'm still very much in the space of relearning who I am in my own physical space as a mom of two—and finding that new self-care routine. This ritual I have shared is the only self-care practice that helps me get away from the chaos of my mind to prioritize my needs.

I hope this practice allows you to give yourself permission to slow down, turn down the volume of your thoughts, create space, and listen to what you need for yourself.

About the Author

TARA HAISLIP

An Intuitive Business Coach, International Bestselling Author, and the CEO of Grounded Energy111, Tara Haislip is a *Woman's Woman in Business*. She helps women find their voices and create a positive work-life balance by managing the details of brand establishment through ghostwriting, copywriting, copy editing, content creation, and building marketing and public relations teams for women-led businesses in the Health and Wellness space.

When not writing for other women, Tara can be found running after her two young boys, showing her love through cooking, and nurturing her self-care practices for a healthy work-life balance that best meets her needs.

Tara has been featured in publications such as Women Thrive Magazine, Best Holistic Life Magazine, Pretty Women Hustle, Medium, GirlBoss, and many more.

To learn more about Tara visit www.groundedenergy111.com and follow her on Instagram @grounded_energy111.

The Sacred Stories

TO UNVEIL YOUR AUTHENTIC VOICE AND JOURNEY

WHAT TO EXPECT from the Ritual/Practice:

Get ready to dive deep into the very essence of who you are. This practice is about asking those soul-stirring questions that make you pause and reflect. It's a time to honor and embrace every twist, turn, and serendipitous moment that has led you to this exact moment.

Have you ever paused to wonder: What is my soul's mission statement? What are the "talking points" of my life's brand story?

We're going to uncover the stories that have shaped you—the big, life-altering moments, as well as the smaller, yet just as significant, experiences. You will connect the dots between your wildest dreams, your core being, and the threads that bind it all together.

Materials/Supplies Needed:

- Journal or Notebook
- Pen or Pencil
- Comfortable Space
- Open Heart and Mind

With these essentials, you're ready to dive deep into your soul's journey.

Time to Complete the Ritual:

The approximate duration needed to complete the ritual is two hours. It's a dedicated time for introspection and exploration that allows you to delve deep into your sacred stories and soul's journey.

Optimal Time to Perform Ritual:

Perform this ritual on a day when you have ample time, ideally with at least two hours to fully engage. Choose a moment when you can set aside distractions and allow yourself the freedom to delve deeply into your soul's journey without interruption. Any day can be perfect for this sacred exploration, as long as you create a nurturing environment conducive to reflection and self-discovery.

Best Time of Year to Perform Ritual:

The ritual can be particularly potent and relevant during times of transition, such as the changing of seasons or significant personal milestones. Ultimately, it's what feels right for you. So, consider doing it during a time when you're seeking deeper introspection and connection with your soul's journey and story.

Description of Ritual

This ritual is a transformative journey into the essence of your life's narrative. It's about discovering the profound talking points that shape your story, and infusing your conversations with depth and resonance. By reflecting on these meaningful moments, you'll breathe life into your interactions, introductions, and personal branding. Ultimately, this practice aims to make you memorable and adored, and deeply connected to yourself as you authentically share the essence of your journey with others

• Find a comfortable, sacred space where you can focus without distractions.

• Read each question and let the answers flow without hesitation. Whatever comes through is meant to be written down. Don't second-guess the thoughts that arise. There is no "right way" to do this. Remember, this is just a rough draft—a starting point. Over the following days, weeks, and months, you'll want to polish this into a succinct and compelling narrative.

SACRED STORY #1: LIFE-ALTERING MOMENTS

Life-Altering Moments are the pivotal turning points in our lives where everything changes. They encapsulate the essence of who we are, our resilience, and our capacity for growth. While we typically experience only a few of these moments in a lifetime, identifying them is crucial for our personal and professional development. These moments can be filled with such shame, heartache, grief, and turmoil that we hide them away and rarely speak of them. But in reality, they are the moments that shape us and our journey, and deserve to be shared. From moments of triumph to unexpected challenges, these stories create intimacy and trust.

A life-altering moment happened when I was preparing for one of the biggest up-levels of my life. I was in the process of transitioning my virtual assistant agency to a publishing company when my husband of twenty-four years said he wanted a divorce; he wasn't interested in counseling or trying to reconcile. To say the rug was pulled out from under me is an understatement—and I landed hard.

I spent the next year focusing on my self care, and prioritizing myself for the first time in my adult life. Openly sharing my experience on social media, in person, and in networking events was my main form of marketing. This effectively brought in my perfect, soul-aligned clients and created a profitable first year, while I prioritized my healing journey and created a new trajectory for my life and business.

• In four-to-six sentences, capture your own Life-altering Moment. Don't worry about the back story, just dive into that defining moment when the ground shifted beneath your feet and changed the course of your life forever. In a few sentences, encapsulate that pivotal moment and the profound impact it had on you.

By asking and answering deeply meaningful questions about these life-altering moments, we can uncover the essence of our journey and infuse our conversations, branding, and interactions with depth and resonance.

SACRED STORY #2: OUR INWARD FACING WHY

Our Inward Facing Why is the heartbeat of our journey—it's deeply personal and fuels our passion. When we ponder the question: Why do you do what you do? we often find deeply personal motivations at the core. Whether it's to create, pursue a passion, or fulfill a desire, these reasons serve as the foundation of our journey. Our Inward Facing Why is intrinsic to our own sense of purpose; it drives us forward even when others may not fully grasp its significance.

• Sum up your driving force in one sentence: "I do what I do because…'"

Recognizing and embracing our Inward Facing Why enables us to align our actions with our deepest values and aspirations, which guided us towards fulfillment and authenticity in all our pursuits. Remember, your Inward Facing Why encapsulates the essence of your work and business, and defines your purpose in a single potent sentence

I do the work I do so I can use my creative expression, wisdom, and expertise to create a life and business I don't need a vacation from.

• Craft this into a mantra, and consistently weave it into your bio, website, resume, and introductions. Make it a habit to share this one-liner within the first three minutes of meeting someone, during videos, interviews, training, and more. By doing so, you'll distinguish yourself and leave a lasting impression.

SACRED STORY #3: -OUR OUTWARD FACING WHY

In one-to-three sentences write your Outward Facing Why.While our Inward Facing Why is personal, our Outward Facing Why is about making a difference in the world. Think of your Outward Facing Why as your mission, or the movement you're creating. This narrative should articulate both the challenge you're addressing and the solution you provide.

I want you to remember how your work contributes to making the world a better place. Recognizing the ongoing impact of your efforts fosters a deeper reverence for the work you do, not just on special occasions, but every single day.

Here are two examples from my own journey that I'd like to share with you:

I support multi-passionate, heart-centered, and growth-driven entrepreneurs in crafting their stories, expertise, and experiences. Through books and media, we ensure our impact extends beyond ourselves and our businesses, combating the sea of online sameness.

- *Problem: The sea of online sameness*
- *Solution: Crafting stories and wisdom that leave a legacy and impact through books and media.*

Creative entrepreneurs often feel constrained by conventional business models and narrow marketing tactics. I empower multi-passionate, heart-centered individuals to break free and authentically share their stories, wisdom, and expertise. By doing so, they leave a lasting impact and legacy.

- *Problem: Stifling business models*
- *Solution: Authentic storytelling in business*

Every single day, remind yourself that the world is brighter because of the work you're putting out there. Take some time to really hone in on your Outward Facing Why, and don't be shy about sharing it with the world. Think of it like your own personal lighthouse guiding others to you—it's what attracts collaboration opportunities and connects you with those who share your mission.

SACRED STORY #4: -TRANSFORMATIVE TWISTS AND TURNS

Explore the intricacies of your journey as we delve into the twists and turns that have shaped your path. Reflect on the defining moments, shake-ups, awakenings, and pattern-interrupts that have led you to where you are today. These experiences, while perhaps not as monumental as our life-altering moments, are nonetheless significant in their impact on your journey.

• Write about this in one-to-three sentences.

Here are two of my twists and turns:

I was juggling a nine-to-five job while caring for my six-year-old daughter, who was battling crippling anxiety that made her physically sick. When my boss refused to accommodate my family's needs, I took charge and launched my own virtual assistant business. This leap not only gave me the flexibility to care for my daughter but also empowered me to find a better work-life balance

In my journey as a virtual assistant, a simple online networking event changed everything. When I shared my work and who I supported, the facilitator saw a connection: "I teach women how to start publishing houses, and they might need your help." From there, I found myself exclusively assisting female-owned publishing ventures, eventually leading me to start my own.

Throughout our lives, we typically encounter six-to-twelve significant shakeups. Take a moment to identify these pivotal moments in your own life. As you begin to connect these shake ups with the life-altering moments, a clearer picture of your life story will emerge. Piece by piece, your unique journey will reveal itself. These moments serve to connect us to one another and reveal the authenticity of our shared human experience through our individual journeys.

Share the Experience:

For the longest time, I felt like I was just another face in the crowd, blending into the familiar landscape of my hometown. Married young, raising my daughters, and navigating through a routine-driven career, my life seemed like a series of checkboxes with little excitement or distinction. Disconnected from my own sense of purpose and identity, I found myself echoing the beliefs of those around me. Yet upon reflection, I discovered recurring themes of grit, determination, curiosity, and a love for adventure woven throughout my experiences. I realized that we don't need dramatic events to define our journey; it's in recognizing the subtle moments and embracing our unique qualities that we find our true story. It's not about being the most successful or glamorous, but about sharing our authentic selves to connect with others and inspire them. By acknowledging these themes, we awaken our spirit and illuminate the richness of our lives.

I encourage you to dive deep into your own sacred stories and uncover the truths hidden within your experiences. Embrace the craziness of life with reverence, and authentically share more of yourself with the world. I promise, this practice will leave you feeling deeply connected to yourself and others—making you feel more alive and vibrant than you have in quite some time.

About the Author

NICOLETTE HALLADAY

Nicolette Halladay thrives on meaningful conversations and an authentic approach to business. As the visionary behind Inspired Hearts Publishing and host of the Radiant Reach Podcast, she's more than a CEO and storyteller—she's a catalyst for transformation. Guiding heart-centered entrepreneurs, she empowers them to craft impactful narratives that amplify their influence.

A personal upheaval was the impetus for Nicolette's journey from virtual assistant to publisher, and also sparked the desire for personal and professional growth and self-discovery. Through encouraging authenticity and resilience, she inspires others to embrace their stories and connect with the world. By supporting entrepreneurs to share their message through a variety of forms of media, she helps them amplify their influence and make a meaningful impact.

Embracing life's adventures with her three wild and wonderful daughters, this Colorado native is a lover of all things outdoors and passionate about connecting with others.

CONNECT WITH NICOLETTE:
• website: www.nicolettehalladay.com
• The Radiant Reach Podcast: Empowered Conversations for Inspired Living

- linkedin: www.linkedin.com/in/nicolette-halladay111
- Instagram: www.instagram.com/nicolettehalladay111

Intentional Sacred Living

CREATE A PORTABLE ALTAR OF YOUR SACRED LIFE

WHAT TO EXPECT from the Ritual/Practice:

What would your life look like if everything in it was infused with sacredness, and you perceived the divinity in yourself and everyone else?

In this ritual, we will explore the theme of living a sacred life with intention, through the process of inquiry, creativity, and vibration, and get clarity on four aspects of your Sacred Life—Sacred Self, Sacred Loves, Sacred Practices, and Sacred Work.

Materials/Supplies Needed:

For the visioning:

- A fragrant flower (rose, jasmine, gardenia) or essential oil
- Journal
- Pen
- Comfortable space, preferably in nature

For creating the watercolor altar:

- Watercolor paper (75lb or more) 9in x 12in or larger

- Watercolor paints in a rainbow of colors
- A couple of brushes
- A palette or small paper plate
- Jar of water
- Paper towel
- Sharpies

Time Needed to Complete the Ritual:

From 60 mins to several hours

Optimal Time of Day to Perform Ritual:

This ritual is best done when you feel relaxed, perhaps in the morning before your daily routine takes over, or when you have some spaciousness during the day.

Best Time of Year to Perform Ritual:

This ritual is ideal to do when you are going through any of these situations:

• During a time of transition or when you are at crossroads, when your role, career or relationship is changing, moving to a new place

• Personal milestones like your birthday, to set forth a new vision of yourself

• Thresholds of energy change, like New Year or a festival that holds personal significance

• Potent cosmic portals like equinox, solstice, new/full moons, eclipses, or when your natal chart is being activated by a transit, awakening a new energy within you.

• Any time you want to get clarity on your path ahead and create the next phase of your life with intention

Purpose:

What if 100% of my life was infused with the energy of sacredness?

This question popped into my mind in March 2021, as I made a big career transition from engineer to coach. While I was already pursuing the sacred life, having all of my life resonating with it seemed out of reach.

We take it for granted that aspects of life will be unpleasant and, over a lifetime, even come to accept or expect it. But being an Aquarian, I've had a hard time following the well-worn path, and during my midlife awakening, I learned how much power a well-crafted intention can have on shifting my reality.

So I carefully examined each area of my life and became clear on my deepest priorities—those that matched who I was becoming, not who I had been.

I identified areas of my life that meant much, and others that were on autopilot. I realized that to create everything with intention, it had to have deep meaning for me. It's not easy to be intentional when you're on autopilot or living parts of your life as dead space. If I didn't honor that part of my life with reverence, it was hard to be conscious while living it.

How did I want to show up for my life, my loved ones as well as my sacred purpose?

This is how Intentional Sacred Living was born.

My wish is that you too will use this ritual to "clear the clutter" and hone into how you want to live this precious life, honor the sacredness within, and align with your highest purpose as a blessing to all of creation.

Benefits:

This practice will help you get a clear vision for four areas of your Sacred Life—Self, Loves, Practices, and Work

Some possible benefits are:

• Get to the truth of who you are, what matters to you most, and how you want your life to look and feel

• Get in touch with your sacred self, and treat yourself with reverence, love, and respect

• Have clarity when faced with multiple choices because the false stuff falls away

• Be able to focus and prioritize the things that are important to you

• Navigate changing times with grace, because you trust yourself, your inner guidance, and your ability to walk in the unknown

• Show up for others in your life with impeccable honor

• Live a life aligned with your higher life purpose because your work expresses your truth

Symbolism or Meaning:

Two symbols in this ritual that hold deep meaning are the *bird cardinal* and the *pink climbing rose*. The cardinal shares that it's time for you to joyfully sing out loud your gifts and your soul song with confidence, and the rose holds a deep connection to the divine creator accessed from within your heart. The fragrance of the rose activates cellular memory of the high vibration of love. You will feel the love of your sacred self as you breathe in the fragrance. We also tone the sacred sound "AUM" to activate the sacred altar.

Personalization:

You may adapt this ritual to areas of life that have personal meaning for you. The creative part of the ritual works with a paper folded twice to create four sides, one for each area. You can use a larger paper to make space for more areas. Instead of the rose, you may use flowers like jasmine, gardenia or lilac, all of which can give you access to a more expansive sense of self as you breathe in the fragrance.

Steps or Process:

This ritual has three parts. We start by connecting to a vision of your sacred self, then journal on the four areas to get clarity, and finally create the watercolor altar of your sacred life.

PART 1. CONNECT TO THE VISION OF YOUR SACRED SELF

Find a comfortable place where you will be undisturbed for this meditation. A place in nature is ideal. If you have access to a rose or essential oil, have that on hand.

Set an intention to meet your Sacred Self.

Place the rose on your heart, or dab a drop of essential oil on the skin around your heart area.

Drop into your heart; breathe slow and deep. Allow the field around your heart to expand.

See and feel a ball of light like the sun, deep in the center of your heart space.

Feel the pristine purity, radiance and warmth of this beautiful light.

With every breath, see this light expand. It grows bigger and infuses every cell of your body with crystalline clarity.

Now see this light projected in front of you—like a big, golden, round doorway. And with a deep breath, step into this doorway into the other side.

Here, you see a beautiful, sacred garden. Pause here for a moment and take in its beauty. You see colorful plants, vibrating with pristine life force energy. You see roses, shrubs and climbers, radiating peace, grace, beauty, and divine presence. You see tall trees and a lovely waterfall with pure flowing water. It has just rained and washed everything with nourishing water. You inhale the freshness of the air and the divine fragrance of roses. You are completely relaxed and at peace.

Now, as you walk through the garden exploring with curiosity, you hear a bird singing out. It's a cardinal. You follow its sweet singing voice through the garden, taking a winding path that goes deeper inside.

And there you see the bird perched on a beautiful, pink, climbing rose bush resplendent with huge, pink roses. There is a bench underneath it and you feel the cardinal is inviting you to take a seat.

So you do. You feel the magnificent presence of this rose being, and you acknowledge it with a loving pulse from your heart.

As if in answer, the rose being showers you with fragrant pink petals and droplets of water. It's raining rose petals on you, evoking a feeling of delight and joy!

As you sit there underneath this climbing rose, breathe in the fragrance. The rose asks you telepathically, *Who do you desire to be, dear one?*

A bit surprised at this question, you realize you do have a choice; it's up to you to decide WHO you want to be going forward. You need not be limited by the past. So you settle in under the rose and tune in deep into your heart.

The clean, clear fragrance of the rose gives you access to a feeling of pure authentic expression of the divine. With every fragrant breath, you go deeper and deeper into the essence of your sacred being.

You feel the vibration, the fragrance of the rose infusing into every cell of your body, clearing away all that is false and revealing your authentic presence.

You feel a sense of lightness and spaciousness as if all that was weighing you down has simply dissolved. Effortlessly.

Bathed in the high vibration of this rose you feel fortified by your own sacred presence, and possibilities open up in your heart and life.

Take your time here. Spend as much time as you feel like and when you are ready, give the cardinal and rose a heartfelt thank you.

She responds with another shower of petals.

Taking a petal with you, you return the way you came, back through the golden door and into your heart and body.

Open your eyes and ground by touching the earth.

Jot down any insights, images, colors, symbols that appeared to you in the vision. These will go into the altar.

PART 2. JOURNAL ON YOUR SACRED LIFE

While holding onto the vibration of expansion experienced during the vision, journal on each part of your life, to get clarity on how you would like to experience it. Jot down key words that encapsulate that energy.

Sacred Self:

Tune into what "sacred" means to you.

• If you acknowledged the divinity within you with reverence, and treated yourself with love, honor and respect in every moment, what would that feel like? What would your most expansive, free Self feel like?

• What would you say "yes" to and "no" to?

• How would you speak and think about yourself and others?

• What strengths and unique gifts would you have the courage to share?

Feel into what aspects, qualities, or identity within you wants to grow in the coming year.

• How will you cultivate this authentic relationship with yourself?

Sacred Loves:

Who are the loved ones who share your life?

Imagine that you empower them to live their highest soul expression with joy.

• If you were to hold a field of impeccable love and honor for these sacred loves, how would you show up?

• How would you speak to them? What thoughts would arise when you think of them? What would you do to support them?

• How will you cultivate this relationship to reflect your divinity and theirs?

Sacred Work:

• What were you born to do?

• What work is your Sacred Self doing and how is it in service to something greater than you?

• If your work was an expression of your unique beautiful nature, what is being expressed?

• How do you feel when you express it?

• What are you curious about exploring at this stage in your life? Curiosity about new topics is a clue to what new aspects of you want to come through.

• What higher skills would you cultivate that allows your sacred purpose to be expressed with joy?

• Who is the receiver of the gift of offering that your sacred work is?

• What is the legacy of your Sacred Self?

Sacred Practices:

Practices done consistently, that honor the sacred nature within, are the structure that hold the new you.

• What is currently part of your daily routine that does not honor your sacred life?

• What support does your heart, body, mind, soul need at this point of time in your life?

• How can you add this to your daily routine to nourish the sacred nature within you to grow?

PART 3. CREATE A WATERCOLOR ALTAR OF YOUR SACRED LIFE

1. Blessing: The watercolor paper is the altar that holds the intention of your sacred life. Bring your hands to your heart to connect with your vision. Then rub your hands on the paper, infusing the vibration of sacredness into it by blessing it. You may also dip a flower in the water jar and gently rub it across the paper, lovingly inviting it to hold your intention.

2. Connect to your vision from the meditation. Allow the vibration you felt to wash over you. Now pick two to three colors intuitively. Lighter colors are preferred as you will be writing on this later in the ritual.

3. Create a wash on one side with the colors you picked, letting your hand move as it wishes to. Let this be a meditative exercise.

4. While the paper dries, create an outline in your journal for how you will fill up the altar. For each of the four areas, write down a word or

phrase that encapsulates the feeling you desire to experience. Draw symbols that came up or have meaning for you. Get clear on what you are willing to release to live that vision, and one action step to build the vision.

5. When the side is dry, paint the other side of the paper intuitively. Continue to journal as this side also dries.

6. When both sides of the paper are dry, fold it along the length, into two. You now have four parts—two in the front and two in the back.

7. With a Sharpie, write the titles on the top of each part (Sacred Self, Sacred Loves, Sacred Work, Sacred Practices).

8. Draw symbols, write key words, spend time decorating, while at the same time feeling into your sacred life. Allow for playfulness and joy as you add your creative energy to your vision.

9. Finally, bring the altar to your heart, step into your Sacred Self, and from this space, sing out "A-U-M" (aaaah ooooh mmmmm) as a way to activate the energy of the creation with sound.

10. Keep this altar in a sacred space and connect with its energy every day.

11. Notice what shows up in your life. What are you prompted to release? What are you guided to do? Take action on the insights as that will align your life to your vision.

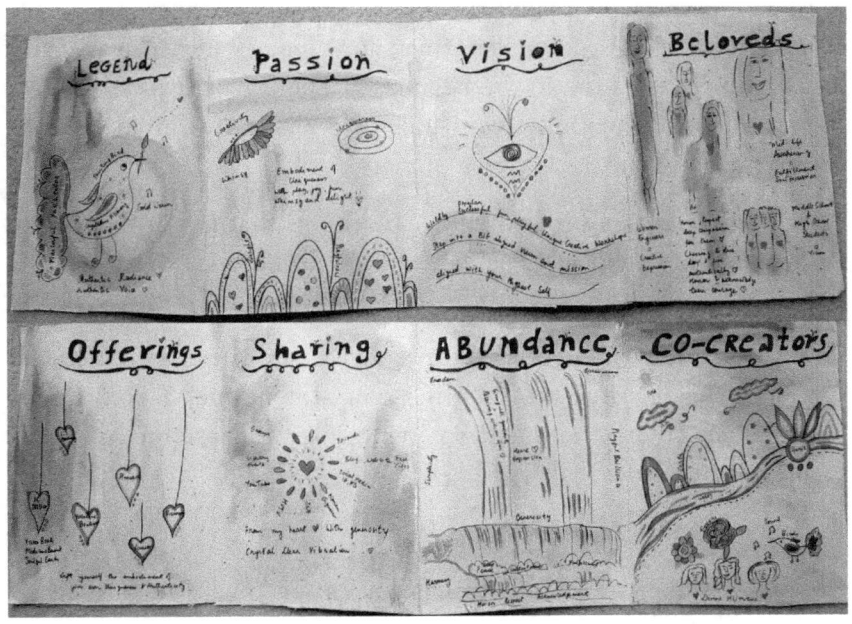

Follow the QR code for a 30 minute video that walks you through the Intentional Sacred Living Ritual; includes a guided rose meditation to connect to your Sacred Self and step by step guide to creating your watercolor altar.

Share the Experience:

When you first do this ritual, it is possible that you may feel disappointment, especially if you have to make a lot of changes in your life to align to sacredness. That is normal; don't judge where you are. This was my experience too in the beginning. There will always be space for refining and upgrading your life. Take it one area at a time; one action step at a time.

Start by first clearing the way. Release things that get in the way of your sacred life, with honor and gratitude for their lessons Then add new aligned actions.

Repeat this ritual often, several times a year and you may notice that you uplevel your life with each iteration. Intentional Sacred Living takes consistent commitment to living your highest life, and gets easier the more you do it.

Reflect on the Impact:

Doing this ritual consistently brings you closer to who you are meant to become. As you make changes to these four areas, how you show up for yourself deepens and strengthens—and this uplevels other areas of your life. It can have a healing effect on your relationships and increase vital life force energy as your work aligns to your highest purpose. Falseness may fall away as a result. It becomes easier to say "no" to the things that are unaligned and "yes" to those that are.

This is a ritual I do often, as it keeps me aligned to my core values and creates simplicity that allows for beauty and grace to flow easily into my life. May this ritual reveal to you your highest path, and may you have the courage to live it with joy!

About the Author

SWATI KAMESWAR

Swati Kameswar is a Visionary Coach, Astrologer, and Artist who helps women in their thirties, forties, and fifties transform the disillusionment of midlife crisis into midlife awakening, by activating their authentic voice and setting up the next phase of life for joyful success. She specializes in helping women develop the power of their voice and speak with personal authority.

A former engineer for two decades, Swati is now known for brilliantly blending transformational coaching with Astrology and Intentional Creativity.

Swati is the creator of "Power of Balance" – an out-of-the-box process that decodes the hidden clues in your natal chart and activates your unique hidden skills that awaken during midlife.

Her wildly popular courses and creative workshops uncover playful brilliance, aliveness, and joy that spills into your life and career!

Download her free gift "12 Paths to Impeccable Personal Power" a toolkit for activating the twelve unique frequencies of your authentic voice, at:

www.activateyourtruthandpower.com/gifts

A Daily Practice

SEVEN KEYS IN CONSCIOUS SOUL REGROUPING FOR THE SACRED SELF

WHAT TO EXPECT **from the Ritual/Practice:** *Begin and end your day consciously mastering your own unique energy.*

The intention of conscious soul regrouping is to have a roadmap to be able to direct and set your energy each day—so you know where you begin energetically, and end energetically. The purpose of this practice is to become more masterful of who you are.

Through my work with clients, I have learned that most of us don't have a "roadmap" to set our energy or regroup from all we have experienced during our day. I realized that when I wrote things down with a pen and paper, I actualized my life more effectively—I had better experiences, or more clearly understood what I was going through.

Having a blueprint to begin and end each day is like having a magic crystal that gives insight into what you're doing here, and is a template for self-discovery. It fills the holes in your spiritual understanding of yourself, taking you from "not knowing" to "knowing." You are here on Planet Earth, so why not make the most of your time well spent.

Doing this daily practice has helped give structure to my life. I have gone from having my energy being wishy-washy all day, or all month, to being proactive, clear, and directed in what I want. I prefer the latter—and so do my clients once they start using it.

What you will need:

• A favorite journal of your choice. I prefer 8x11 with big spaces in-between.

• Your favorite writing tools: colored pencils, ink pens, or—my personal favorite—colored gel pens to make things more interesting and fun.

The time you will need is up to you: I suggest fifteen or thirty minutes, every morning and evening.

The purpose of this practice is to become more masterful in understanding yourself and what your spiritual journey can be. By consciously setting your energy in the morning, then spiritually regrouping your energy at the end of the day, you will have the ability to learn, grow, and discover through a mindful approach. This ritual will guide you, as an individual, to become aware of the choices you have. It is a blueprint to being the master of your own ship.

What will happen as you make this a daily practice? You'll gain clarity on how you want to see, feel, and hear the world around you. You'll become connected to your inner wisdom and higher self. And you will foster a divine connection that will enhance you emotionally, mentally, and spiritually.

"You came to Planet Earth to find yourself. Happiness, success, and abundance are already yours. All you need to do is become a master of yourself." - *Francisco Coll D.D.*

You are a soul with a body traveling physically here on Planet Earth. You came for a reason; making good use of your time while here is important. This simple, practical, habit will give you daily keys to unlock who you truly are, and understand what you are working through and what you are working towards. It will be a guideline in your spiritual journey to what you want to gain and discover while being here.

SEVEN MORNING SOUL CONSCIOUS KEYS:

This morning practice is a way to set your energy each day.

First Key: Set the mood. Light a candle. Light *Goloka Archangel Divine Incense* or burn your favorite sage. Play soft music if you prefer. If desired, have your most treasured morning beverage nearby.

Now imagine a crystal clear, divine, white light coming from the universe, spiritually cleansing you from your head to your feet. If you desire, ask your spiritual guidance to join you at this time. If anything from your sleep needs to be released, it is transformed by the light. See, feel, and experience your body being spiritually cleansed and cleared with the divine, white light.

Now imagine that divine, white light caressing the space you're in. Cleansing it, going out into your city, state/province, country, and around the world. Send a vibration of love, healing, and cleansing to all who exist on this planet. Now send this light of cleansing back to yourself. Feel spiritually cleansed. Open your eyes with positive energy.

After spiritually cleansing yourself and your environment, ask your higher self/guidance/inner wisdom to give you a keyword for the day. The first word you experience comes from your guidance/higher self. It is instantaneous. Take a deep breath, release the breath and allow the word to come to mind. Write it down. This keyword is your spiritual pivot point for the day.

Your guidance/higher self/inner wisdom has the "big picture" of your plan/purpose in life. Trust that the first word you receive is allowing that part of yourself to come to focus. This word may be weird, unusual, or simple. It doesn't matter.

Do not analyze, dissect, or change your first word. It's there for a reason. Once you have written your keyword, make a keyword sentence out of the word.

Example: Keyword - Alarm

Keyword Sentence: I become aware of any spiritual alarms throughout my day.

Another Example: Keyword - Cheer

Keyword Sentence: I cheer myself and others forward with enthusiasm.

Second Key: Ask, *"What am I happy about in my life today?"* All of us can have up-days and down-days. This question is to guide you on a positive focus each day while going through the challenges you may face. It helps you to see there is light in darkness, such as illness, death, or grief. I can be happy with my favorite cup of coffee, food in the fridge, and the sun shining.

Third Key: Ask, *"How do I want to feel today?"* This helps you realize you can make a conscious choice in how you want to feel. One can be miserable for three minutes or thirty years. By choosing this feeling, you recognize how much power you have in your positive feelings.

Fourth Key: Ask, *"What will I improve upon today?"* This could be personal, material, spiritual, or emotional needs. It could relate to anything from getting the stains out of a T-shirt, to fixing something, or learning to quiet the "monkey mind." No matter what it is, this keeps your energy moving forward, rather than being stuck.

Fifth Key: Ask, *"What goals will I take action on today?"* Goals can be broken down into steps. Each step completes the goal. I prefer one-to-three goals so I don't feel overwhelmed.

Example: Perhaps you want to spend more time with family and friends. What steps will help you in this goal? You could create a

Potluck dinner once a week for everyone to socialize. Or host a monthly movie or game night at home.

Another Example: Might be organizing your house/living space. The steps could be picking up groceries, doing laundry, or vacuuming the floor.

Creating easy, simple steps allows you to accomplish your goal. Make it a fun adventure. In this way you will feel fulfilled, no matter what goal you are working on.

Sixth Key: Ask, *"What choices will help me align with my soul's purpose?"* This is often a feeling deep inside; you already know, naturally, what that is. This feeling is also changeable because the evolution of your soul is growing. What you would have felt a decade ago will, perhaps, be different now. During each seven-year-cycle, you are automatically changing your state of consciousness. Life moves in rhythms.

Examples: Daring yourself to go live on Instagram/social media channels to promote yourself or something you do. Changing careers. Or taking your first international trip.

Seventh Key: This is where the magic is! Sit quietly for three-to-five minutes. Close your eyes and take a deep breath. Release the breath out. Ask your higher self or guidance to come close.

Now, visualize all those things you wrote that you're happy about. Add anything else you see, feel, or hear. Imagine improving your purpose for the day and meeting any goals you have. Align into your soul's purpose in the here and now. See, feel, and hear anything that makes that real inside your mind. Make it vivid. Colorful. Your mind is a data machine willing to help you upgrade its software.

Imagine, visualize, and accept whatever happens with your day. You have incredible power to work with your guidance, the universe, in manifesting a beautiful life of your creation.

Now bring that divine, white light around you once more, cleansing you from your crown through your body, and out the bottom of your feet. Sense that you are 100% energetically cleansed. You can ask your angels/guidance to help you also; allow yourself that extra backing from your support team.

You are now spiritually ready for your day!

Go out into your world knowing you have set your energy to take action into your day.

SEVEN EVENING SOUL CONSCIOUS KEYS IN REGROUPING YOUR DAY

First Key: Ask, *"How did my Keyword/Keyword Sentence fit with my day?"*

It is important to understand how your day and your inner wisdom are always working together for you.

Second Key: Ask, *"What did I learn about myself today spiritually, physically, mentally/emotionally, or anything else that may fit?"*

Third Key: Ask, *"What was the best part of my day?"*

Fourth Key: Ask, *"What did I accomplish today?"*

Fifth Key: Ask, *"Was I loyal and honest to my own needs and wants today? If not, why?"*

Sixth Key: Ask, *"In what ways would I have done anything different today?"*

Seventh Key: Spiritually release the day by cleansing yourself and your environment with the white light, as you did in the morning. For three-to-five minutes, visualize the good things you desire for tomorrow. Before retiring for bed, perhaps think about all the good things from your day and bring them into your next day, if needed. You can ask your higher self for three good feelings you desire for the next day that you also want to have in your tomorrow; already believing you can have that if you want it.

This routine has helped me go from being in a rut to being unstuck. Rather than struggling with no energy, I now receive energy freely. Practicing this ritual has led me to a place where I can write down feelings or emotions to live uplifting days, rather than spend too many days down in a funk. Now, I am able to discern what is leading me to learn and grow. Living life in a physical body on Planet Earth isn't alway a joyride. Having this system has helped me, and my clients, to live more authentically in what we want out of life; every day we overcome challenges to rise above the fray.

By utilizing *The Seven Keys in Soul Conscious Regrouping*, you'll begin to understand how you have choices in setting your energy each day. This regroups:

• What you have learned and received from your daily experiences.

• How you can do things differently. Knowing and understanding what you will do differently helps you reset your experiences, so you do not repeat them. This is because you have regrouped within your-self and learned the spiritual lesson of it.

This ritual gives you insight and inspiration, and allows you to re-adjust what is needed. It brings healing, a deeper connection to oneself, and a long-lasting practice that you will continue to use for decades to come.

At the end of each month you can go back through your pages and regroup your monthly experiences. This includes:

• What you achieved and accomplished that month.

• What you have learned or improved upon. Taking time to under-stand what you are going through, what you are gaining from the growth, and getting insights, sets you propelling in motion.

• Your daily best highlights. Acknowledging the good of your day is important so you recognize the positive aspects that happen that may be unbeknown at the time.

Spiritually, a soul needs to regroup daily, weekly, and monthly. Using this system is a blueprint in mastering your energy each day, week, and month. Everyday, you become more and more masterful of your spiritual nature. By following this ritual, you will develop your personal roadmap in what you are gaining from your earthly experience, and create your best life. This will guide you to reap the rewards of all that you came here to learn, before you return to the ALL, your true home.

> *"Every lifetime is an opportunity to become more masterful of your energy. What you master today, you will reap in rewards for yourself—tomorrow and into your future."*

-April Azzolino

Follow the QR code to Listen to Meet Your Primary Angel Meditation by April Azzolino on #SoundCloud
Connect with one of your primary angelic guides for insights and inspiration.

About the Author

APRIL AZZOLINO

April Azzolino guides modern women to discover their own spiritual mysteries of life, inspiring them to live a self-directed life. Trained as an International Spiritual Certified Instructor/Consultant with Wayshowers College, she employs unique methods to enhance a woman's life through Private Spiritual Mentoring Sessions, Psychic Development, Spiritual Hypnosis, Childhood Chakra Regression, and Past Life Explorations.

Making the mysteries of life answerable is April's driving force. Her clients find healing, spiritual direction, and answers that they never had before. Balancing their intellectual and unconscious mind, her clients move from being stuck to unstuck.

April's article "Magic number 7" is featured in Breathe Magazine, Issue #42. In 2022, her chapter "Trusting My Inner Knowing" was published in the multi-author book *The Voyage and The Return*.

April lives in Las Vegas, Nevada with her husband. When she's not working, you'll find her in the kitchen cooking something scrumptious or watching a sunset glow.

Ask April for complimentary consultation or read her spiritual blogs for your pleasure, https://www.aprilazzolino.com/blog/

Contact details: april@aprilazzolino.com

Holistic Healing for Mind, Body, and Soul

A JOURNEY OF FORGIVENESS AND CLEANSING

THIS PRACTICE ENCOMPASSES two separate rituals: one of **forgiveness** and one of **cleansing**.

Forgiveness:

One effective method of forgiveness is through a *letter-writing and burning ceremony*.

The act of writing and burning a letter is an ancient ritual that has been utilized for centuries as a method to forgive, process emotions, and find closure in challenging situations. This practice is believed to be cathartic, allowing individuals to express their thoughts and feelings on paper, then symbolically release them through burning.

The act of burning the letter is seen as a transformative process, signifying the release of emotional burdens and the beginning of a new chapter. This ritual can provide emotional healing and a sense of closure, allowing individuals to move forward from difficult experiences.

Cleansing:

One effective method of cleansing is through *smudging.*

Smudging is a traditional ceremony practiced by various cultures for purifying or cleansing the soul, as well as clearing negative energy from a person or place. The practice of smudging is deeply rooted in spiritual and cultural traditions and is believed to promote emotional, mental, and spiritual well-being.

1. FORGIVENESS THROUGH A LETTER-WRITING AND BURNING CEREMONY.

1. Purpose

Forgiveness through a letter-writing and burning ceremony allows you to write a private letter to those who have wronged you— expressing all bottled-up emotions, read it aloud, and then burn the letter while reciting forgiveness affirmations as a symbolic act of letting go. This process is a conscious decision to release anger, resentment, guilt about past experiences, and old negative energies, and to invite positivity and new opportunities to your life. It involves making peace with the past to live in peace in the present, and provides a structured approach to expressing and releasing these emotions in a private and cathartic manner.

Forgiveness is a practice that requires dedication and resolve, similar to yoga or meditation. It is a commitment to a new way of life focused on peace and emotional well-being. By allowing yourself the time and space to write down and acknowledge the impact of past experiences, you can begin the process of healing, move forward with clarity, manifest your desires, and achieve emotional well-being.

Forgiveness does not mean forgetting, excusing, or condoning what happened, nor does it require acting like it never occurred. It is not about fixing relationships or including the other person, and it is not done to benefit them, but to free you from negative emotions.

Approach this ritual with self-compassion, mindfulness, intention, and a commitment to your own healing journey. Remember that this process is a personal and introspective practice that aids in processing emotions and finding peace and closure.

2. Symbolism or Meaning

The act of writing letters serves as a powerful means of externalizing and acknowledging our innermost feelings, thoughts, and memories. By putting pen to paper, we transform intangible emotions into tangible and real expressions. This process allows us to honor our experiences and give voice to what lies within us. Writing provides a tangible form for our emotions, as it symbolizes the acknowledgment of our innermost thoughts and feelings. It can be a cathartic and transformative practice that enables individuals to process and externalize their emotions in a meaningful way.

The act of burning the letters symbolizes a release of the pain and hurt we have been holding onto. It allows us to physically let go of our words and emotions, and creates space for healing and transformation.

3. Steps or Process

• Grab a pen/pencil and paper

Pick a form that resonates with you: it may be a fresh sheet of paper, or even a torn page from your journal. Choose something that serves as a visual reminder of what you are releasing.

• Write with passion

Pour your heart out onto the paper for each specific person who has wronged you. Do not filter or judge yourself. Communicate and express exactly how each person made you feel during the relationship, how you feel the way you do, what their actions caused you to experience, the impact they have had on your life, what they have changed, hurt, or broken within you. Write about whatever needs to come forth, whether it is grief, anger, resentment, guilt, forgiveness, unspoken words, or the things that caused you to feel shame, ashamed, stupid, scared, lost, judged, not enough, not loved. Be utterly specific, raw, and authentic. Let her rip!

- **Burn ceremony.**

By yourself, read each letter out loud, letting all the emotions come out. Allow yourself to cry if needed.

Set fire to your letters with a match or lighter and dispose in your safe-burning receptacle or firepit. As you watch the flames burn the paper, repeat these affirming words:

I now release, burn, and clear the lessons of all the negativity, anger, pain, bad feelings, circumstances, experiences, and relationships that were given to me by you in the letter.

I now vow to learn these lessons in a different way, one that feels better and opens my heart.

I also vow to love, respect and care for myself while accepting light, love, peace, compassion, resonance, divine and joy in my life.

<Enter Person's Name>, I forgive you for not being the way I wanted you to be. I forgive you for not understanding. I forgive you for making mistakes. I forgive you for hurting me, yourself, and others. I forgive you for not acting the way you should have acted. I forgive you and I set you free.

Visualize the release of all that no longer serves you and embrace the new beginnings that come with forgiveness and self-care. May you find healing, peace, and a deeper sense of self-love as you continue your journey towards growth and transformation. You are deserving of light, love and all the beauty that life has to offer.

2. Cleansing through Smudging

1. Purpose

Smudging involves burning sacred herbs, such as sage or sweetgrass, and allowing the smoke to waft around the individual or space to promote spiritual cleansing and healing.

Smudging can serve as a powerful tool for spiritual growth, grounding, and centering. It can help individuals release negative energy, open themselves up to healing and positivity, and deepen their connection to the spiritual realm. Through the practice of smudging, one can find a sense of peace, balance, and harmony within themselves and their surroundings.

Whether used for personal reflection, ritual cleansing, or to honor tradition and heritage, smudging holds deep meaning and significance for those who practice it. It serves as a reminder of the sacredness and interconnectedness of all things, and a way to cultivate a sense of reverence and mindfulness in daily life.

2. Symbolism

Smudging represents a beautiful, meaningful, and sacred practice that not only cleanses and purifies but also allows individuals to connect with their spiritual journey, ancestry, and the interconnected web of life. It is a way to honor tradition, cultivate mindfulness, and create a sacred space for spiritual exploration and growth.

3. Steps or Process

• Set Up your Space

Lay out your smudge bowl—an abalone shell or pottery bowl—a feather or hand fan, a bundle of sage or sweetgrass, sand, and matches or a lighter. Fill your shell or bowl with sand. If smudging inside, open all the windows and curtains to allow clean air to enter.

• Light your Bundle

Using matches or a lighter, light your bundle of sage or sweetgrass.

Once lit, use the feather, hand fan, or your hand to direct the sacred smoke towards your entire body, from head to toe and front and back to help set your intentions.

• **Set your Intentions**

To remove all negative energies left after the letter burning ceremony.

To bless your body.

• **Smudging Ceremony**

Keep directing the sacred smoke towards specific parts of your body as you read Grandmother Wapajea Walks on Water's Smudging Prayer:

> May your hands be cleansed, that they create beautiful
>   things.
> May your feet be cleansed, that they might take you
>   where you most need to be.
> May your heart be cleansed, that you might hear its
>   message clearly.
> May your throat be cleansed, that you might speak
>   rightly when words are needed.
> May your eyes be cleansed, that you might see the signs
>   and wonders of the world.
> May this person and space be washed clean by the
>   smoke of this fragrant plant.
> And may that same smoke carry your prayers, spiraling
>   to the heavens.

• **Thank your Creator**

Release everything from the letter burning ceremony and let it all go.

Thank your creator ~ Miigwech

Let the medicine burn out without interference, as this is an important aspect of the smudging ritual. The smoke produced during smudging is believed to be a direct line of communication to the Creator, carrying prayers, intentions, and offerings to the spiritual realm. By letting the herbs burn out naturally, without interruption, it is thought that the connection between the physical and spiritual worlds will remain unbroken. In this way, letting the medicine burn out without interference is a gesture of reverence, trust, and belief in the power of the smudging ritual to connect individuals with the divine and the spiritual realm.

Follow the QR code to be guided through the Smudging Prayer.

<u>Share the Experience:</u>

My healing journey included both rituals as I needed to forgive, let go of many negative emotions and stories, and cleanse my mind, body, and soul.

The letter writing process unleashed so many emotions, thoughts, sensations, and pain that I had kept bottled up for years. Putting pen to paper provided a cathartic, structured approach to vent and be authentic, while allowing me to process and externalize my emotions and feelings in a meaningful way.

I was astonished at the number of pages I wrote; I definitely "let her rip." I did not hold back. I was authentic and raw in my writing, and cried, screamed, and at times, forgot to breathe. Although this was very hard to do, I have to say it was incredibly rewarding. By the end of the third letter, I felt lighter. All the emotions and feelings started to calm down, the pain I was experiencing in my body was slowly leaving, and that night, I slept like a baby.

The letter burning ceremony was highly emotional. I broke down a few times while reading my letters—tears were flowing and my nose was running! I was a hot mess express; I sobbed so much that I became dehydrated. Burning the letters, forgiving, and expressing the affirming words gave me a sense of peace, joy, and relief. The anger, resentment, guilt, and old negative energies dissipated tremendously, and I felt I was ready to let all that go. I felt lighter, and realized that none of these emotions were serving me.

The smudging ceremony was exhilarating. It grounded and centered me, which allowed me to fully release all the negative emotions, feelings, and energies I had been holding on to for many years. By the end of it, I felt fifteen pounds lighter!

Today, I smudge my home, body, mind, and soul at the beginning of every season: spring, summer, fall, and winter.

Both these rituals expedited my journey to growth, transformation, and celebration. Today, nothing holds me back—nor do I keep things bottled up! I'm able to love myself in every way, process any negative emotions, energies, and feelings rather quickly, and move on.

As a life coach, many of my clients go through these two rituals—and they love it. Afterwards, they feel a deeper connection with themselves, and others. Their relationships are meaningful and strong and they are better equipped, emotionally and spiritually, to deal with ongoing daily challenges and release emotions and feelings quickly. These rituals allow them to love themselves completely and move forward with a clear mind and an open heart, ready to embrace whatever comes next in life.

"One of the most courageous decisions you'll ever make is finally letting go of what is hurting your heart and soul."

~ Brigitte Nicole

Miigwech

With gratitude,

Coach Roxy

Helping you Transform & Celebrate Life

Letter Writing	Letter Burning	Smudging
Materials/Supplies Needed: • Pen or Pencils • Paper • Eraser	Materials/Supplies Needed: • Matches or Lighter • Safe Burn-Friendly Receptacle or Fire Pit	Materials/Supplies Needed: • A Smudge Bowl: Abalone Shell or Pottery Bowl • A Feather or Fan • Bundle of Sage or Sweetgrass • Sand • Matches or Lighter
Time Needed to Complete • As long as you need. (I prefer to do it quickly to heal and move on)	Time Needed to Complete • 15 to 30 minutes depending on the number of letters you have.	Time Needed to Complete • As long as you need, usually about 10 minutes
Optimal Time of Day • First thing in the morning	Optimal Time of Day • First thing in the morning, well letter writing is completed.	Optimal Time of Day • First thing in the morning after letter burning is completed.
Best Time of Year • • As required.	Best Time of Year • As required. Following completion of Letter Writing	Best Time of Year • As required. Following Letter Burning

About the Author

ROXY RAPEDIUS

Author Roxy Rapedius is an Executive Mindset and Wellness Coach and CEO of Life Coach with Roxy where she empowers individuals through change, transition, and transformation. With a plethora of experience across many different industries, her current focus is to help people realize their spiritual tools to achieve success.

Passionate and dedicated to enhancing the lives of those she touches by helping them reach their goals, Roxy believes that wellness matters in every aspect of our life: physical health, environmental (including home, community, and the world itself), personal/work life, and financial.

Published in Brainz Magazine and by Inspired Hearts Publishing, Roxy has a curiosity and keen desire to further expand her knowledge and acumen to reach greater heights in serving others as a leader in business and life.

As an established leader who gets results, she lives happily with her husband in Hamilton, Ontario, Canada.

You can visit her online at:
https://www.wellnesswithroxy.com
https://linktr.ee/lifecoachwithroxy
https://www.facebook.com/lifecoachwithroxy

Embracing the Shakti Within

ANCESTRAL WISDOM FOR TODAY'S WOMAN

EMBRACING THE SHAKTI WITHIN: Ancestral Wisdom for Today's Woman

Nestled in the mystical landscapes of India, where the sacred rivers Ganga and Yamuna meander through the ancient terrains, the profound concept of Shakti has been venerated for millennia. Shakti, the divine feminine force, is considered the essence of existence and is deeply integral to Hindu philosophy. In this chapter, we explore how this revered energy is intricately woven into the lives of women today, as it blends timeless traditions with the necessities of modern living, and we reflect on my journey as a woman of Indian origin reconnecting with her roots.

The Essence of Shakti

In Sanskrit, Shakti means "power" or "energy." In the realm of Hinduism, it embodies the dynamic forces that animate the universe. The divine feminine is manifested through various deities such as Durga, the goddess of strength; Kali, the goddess of destruction; Saraswati, the goddess of wisdom; and Lakshmi, the goddess of prosperity. These figures play a pivotal role in Hindu worship, particularly during festivals like Navaratri—a time of devotion and celebration that invites the blessings of these goddesses for strength, protection, and abundance.

The narratives of Shakti, such as those found in the *Devi Mahatmya* of the Markandeya Purana, depict her as the supreme cosmic power. These stories are not just mythological accounts; they are imbued with deep spiritual teachings about the battles against ego and ignorance—challenges that every human being encounters.

Here are some snippets from Hindu mythology that reveal the diverse divine powers of Shakti, showcasing her manifold forms and the unique strengths each embodies.

The Story of Goddess Durga and Mahishasura

The tale of Goddess Durga and the demon Mahishasura embodies the triumph of good over evil. Mahishasura, having received a boon that no man could kill him, unleashed terror upon the earth and heavens. The gods, unable to defeat him, pooled their divine energies to create Goddess Durga. Empowered with multiple arms, each wielding a weapon gifted by various gods, Durga rode into battle on a lion. After a fierce combat, she defeated Mahishasura, symbolizing the victory of divine feminine power over brute strength and ignorance.

The Legend of Sati and the Origin of Shakti Peethas

Sati, the first consort of Shiva, immolated herself in the sacrificial fire to protest her father Daksha's disrespect towards Shiva. Distraught, Shiva carried Sati's body and wandered the universe. To calm him, Vishnu disintegrated Sati's body with his discus, and the parts fell on earth, becoming Shakti Peethas. Each Peetha is a shrine where the divine feminine's energy is believed to be especially potent, illustrating the pervasive presence and influence of Shakti across the cosmos.

The Tale of Saraswati and the Birth of Wisdom

Goddess Saraswati, known as the deity of wisdom, knowledge, and arts, was created by Brahma to bring order to chaos. Saraswati provided the insight needed to understand the nature of reality and the consciousness to perceive the world. Her emergence highlights the essence of Shakti as the source of creativity and intellect, showing how the divine feminine is fundamental to the development of civilization and culture.

Kali's Dance of Destruction and Rebirth

Kali, a fierce manifestation of Goddess Durga, was born from her brow during a battle with demonic forces. As Kali annihilated the demons, her uncontrollable rage led her to dance destructively, threatening the world. Shiva, to stop her, lay beneath her feet, and when Kali realized she was standing on her consort, she calmed down. This story illustrates the balance of creation and destruction inherent in Shakti, highlighting her role in the cycle of life and rebirth.

Lakshmi and the Churning of the Ocean

When the gods and demons churned the ocean of milk to seek the elixir of immortality, many divine objects and beings emerged, including Goddess Lakshmi, the goddess of wealth and prosperity. She chose Vishnu as her consort, symbolizing the alignment of material wealth and spiritual elevation. Lakshmi's emergence from the ocean represents the bounty and nurturing aspect of Shakti, emphasizing her role in sustaining life and civilization.

The Sacred Energy Centers

Central to Shakti worship are the chakras, or energy centers within the body, among which the womb chakra is especially venerated as a significant source of divine feminine power. It is believed that awakening this chakra can enhance spiritual communication and intuition, establishing a direct link to the Divine Mother and fostering the manifestation of divine qualities in daily life.

Throughout the Indian subcontinent, the Shakti Peethas—sacred sites where pieces of the goddess Sati's body are said to have fallen—are considered powerful energy vortexes. These sites serve as pilgrimage destinations that provide devotees with profound spiritual experiences of the divine feminine, resonating deeply with those who visit.

Connecting with Maternal Lineage

Recognizing and embracing one's maternal lineage is crucial for harnessing ancestral wisdom. Our foremothers, carriers of knowledge and resilience, shape not only our genetic makeup but also our spiritual and emotional landscapes. By reconnecting with this lineage, we access a deep reservoir of collective memory and inherited strength, which is essential for our personal growth and spiritual evolution.

Your Everyday Ritual: Awakening the Inner Goddess

This ritual can be personalized to be as simple or as elaborate as you wish. Whether performed upon waking in your bed or more formally in a designated sacred space, the ritual is flexible and guided by your inner self.

Preparing the Sacred Space

If time allows, choose a peaceful spot or set up an altar covered with a red silk cloth, symbolizing divine energy. You may place a statue of the Goddess at the center, surrounded by flowers (preferably red), and light incense and candles. Each element is chosen for its spiritual significance, with their light symbolizing divine presence. Crystals such as Moonstone, Rose Quartz, or Red Jasper can also be used to embody the Goddess's energy.

Time Needed: Approximately 15-30 minutes

Optimal Time of Day: Early morning or evening

The Process

1. As you open your eyes when you wake up, put your palms together and just look at the lines on your palms—acknowledging your own journey embedded there.

2. As you do so, thank your ancestors and spiritual team for being there with you at all times.

3. Slowly take your palm to your womb and place it gently, sensing the energy vortex there.

4. Now, as your palms warm up the energy vortex there, drop your consciousness to your womb. Visualize a luminous orb of light at your womb and feel all the sensations that come up.

5. Expand this orb using your intention and allow it to grow beyond yourself and make it boundless.

6. Think of your mother and foremothers who came before you. Acknowledge each one of them individually for their love, strength, and wisdom. And for having a part of them in you. Sense their presence and blessings.

7. Now acknowledge the most divine form of the Goddess Shakti, ask for her blessings and simply connect with her energies. Enjoy the power and bliss as her energies engulf you.

8. As you do this, sit in meditation to sense what comes up. You can go deeper if you have pressing issues in life and ask for support and guidance—or simply surrender your day to them, asking for their guidance and support.

9. These energies are powerful, so with gratitude slowly center yourself back to your heart space and open your eyes.

10. Remember to ground yourself by drinking water or simply walking barefoot.

What to Expect

When engaging in this ritual, expect to experience a profound sense of connection, empowerment, and spiritual enlightenment. By honoring your ancestors and invoking the presence of Goddess Shakti, you awaken dormant energies within yourself and tap into the timeless power of ancestral knowledge. This practice invites you to turn inward, seeking guidance and strength from within while also fostering a deep connection to the divine feminine. Expect to feel a sense of clarity, purpose, and inner peace as you embark on this journey of self-discovery and empowerment.

My Personal Experience

Growing up in India, I closely observed the invocation of the divine feminine. Although my connection to my divine feminine took time to develop, it eventually blossomed, granting me immense strength and deep wisdom. My experiences as a mother have also shaped my insights into these practices. As I delved deeper into energy healing and spiritual practices I crafted a personal ritual that has become a cornerstone of my daily life, by drawing upon the collective wisdom of my foremothers. This ritual not only serves as a spiritual practice but also as a powerful affirmation of my identity and heritage, allowing me to remain deeply rooted in my culture while navigating the complexities of modern life. Through this practice, I honor the women who came before me, whose resilience and wisdom pulse through my veins. This ritual is a celebration of my lineage, a sacred tradition that reinforces my connection to my Indian roots and the universal energy of Shakti.

Follow the QR code to access "Your Everyday Ritual – Awakening the Inner Goddess."

About the Author

VANDANA SINHA

Vandana Sinha, the learned creator of the "Embrace Your Inner Goddess" ritual, and founder of VanSinha LLC, stands at the vanguard of energy consciousness and spiritual coaching. With over three decades of experience, she specializes in a range of Quantum Energy healing modalities, including Reiki, Pranic Healing, Angel, Healing, Akashic Records, and Theta Healing. Having cultivated a profound understanding of the human energy field as a dynamic reservoir of potential for growth, healing, and manifestation, she uses this knowledge as the base of her spiritual work.

Using her distinctively holistic approach, Vandana blends ancient wisdom with contemporary spiritual insights to guide individuals toward profound healing and self-discovery. Celebrated for her contributions, she has been honored by "Marquis Who's Who" and the "Women of the Decade" award from the Women Economic Forum. As a luminary in spiritual evolution, Vandana's insights have graced *MysticMag* and Jim Masters' CUTV talk show.

Offering a sanctuary of wisdom, Vandana curates soul-enriching workshops and experiences. Nestled in the warmth of Orange County, California, she cherishes life with her family and the serene companionship of her Persian cat.

Connect with Vandana

www.vansinha.com

www.instagram.com/vansinha_coach/

www.linkedin.com/in/vandanasinha/

www.youtube.com/@vansinha_coach

Mindful Hydration For Body, Mind, and Spirit

LIVING in the unforgiving Texas heat as a child, and with the guidance from wise grandmothers, my early years were graced with the blessings of abundant hydration inside and out. Our bodies crave and need this nourishment and cleansing, but throughout my life, I strayed from this life-sustaining wisdom. As a result, my body, mind, and spirit experienced hormonal crashes, organ breakdown, brain fog, fatigue, and bouts of anxiety in each adult decade of my life—until I embraced this life-affirming hydration ritual passed down from my wise grandmothers and their wise ancestors before them. Sometimes the simplest of rituals is overlooked. Fresh water is one of the most powerful and necessary elements on the planet.

Looking back with fondness at my Colombian Grandmother, who was born in 1913 and lived to be ninety-six, I remember as a kid seeing her false teeth in a glass with a cleaning solution. She educated me on the importance of drinking lots of water daily, as she knowingly informed me that soda rots from the inside out. Later, when I was twenty-one, I saw a direct example of this when my future mother-in-law was diagnosed with bone marrow cancer; she was in her early forties and her main source of hydration was cola. Seeing her go through a painful bone marrow transplant, and living fifteen more years on strong pain medication that left her zombie-like, helped me know the importance of not smoking or drinking cola. This belief was reinforced when my sister was diagnosed with cancer in her late forties after a lifelong diet soda and cigarette habit. On top of this, a special client of mine confided in me that she believed her daily diet soda habit was what contributed to her breast cancer diagnosis at age forty. Soon after her diagnosis, she went through chemotherapy and radiation treatments at her doctor's advice, yet no nutrition or hydration advice was recommended. Decades later, she was again diagnosed with cancer and decided to go to an alternative cancer center in the S.W. U.S. The first thing they recommended was that she replace her daily diet soda with a gallon of filtered water, and they also recommended liquid I.V. treatments from their trained nurses.

Working as a massage therapist and health coach has given me direct access to see what healthy hydration feels and looks like in the body. I always talk about healthy hydration and nutrition with my clients who often tell me about their hydration habits. Our daily habits inform our genes, how genes express themselves, and how well the body functions. This is known as Epigenetics: the study of how your behaviors and environment can cause changes that affect the way your genes work. Unlike genetic changes, epigenetic changes are reversible.

I've learned to accept that sometimes people learn too late about how their habits cause dysfunction in the body and receive cancer and/or diabetes diagnoses in their forties—or younger. The body has a filtration system that needs lots of fresh and filtered water, plus minerals, to remove toxins. Signs of dehydration include headache, fatigue, nausea, dizziness, hunger, insomnia, constipation, and muscle cramps. Interestingly, signs of thirst generally occur *after* a person is already dehydrated.

Witnessing clients and family embrace mindful hydration has shown me miracles of migraines and other health issues becoming almost non-existent—unless mindful hydration is mostly ignored for decades. This is why I embrace and advocate living by the "80/20 Rule" of making eighty percent healthy choices and habits regarding personal nutrition and hydration.

Dear One, it is with great joy and sincerity that I pass on this wisdom to future generations. I ask you to keep a curious heart and embrace this life-affirming, foundational ritual I am sharing with you.

Materials Needed:

Filtered water. The daily recommendation by most experts is half your body weight in ounces. A 150-pound person would need about 75oz a day. That's a little more than half a gallon (64oz) a day, or a little less than two liters a day. That's three 24oz water bottles which is very doable with practice and intention. The recommended daily intake to maintain optimal health: Women 2-3 liters, and Men 3-4 liters.

Glass or unlined aluminum or steel water bottles are unlikely to leach chemicals into your filtered water, as most plastics do. Some metal bottles, however, have epoxy linings which may contain BPA or its alternatives.

Other ideas to enhance your hydration experience include:

• A pinch of Celtic salt

• Aloe vera juice

• A teaspoon of Apple Cider Vinegar (which may help boost immunity, break down fat, and help reduce acid reflux)

• A hand citrus press

• Epsom salt

• A reusable straw

• Orange, lemon, lime, ginger root, or cucumber slices, or citrus slices for infused hydration.

LMNT electrolyte drink packets, Ath zero sugar electrolytes, Emergen-C, Cal-Mag, and other electrolyte replacements are also available for your use. Coconut Water is another excellent hydrating choice.

Time Needed:
5 minutes to 1 hour (be flexible and enjoy your daily ritual)

Optimal Time of Day to Perform Ritual:
Upon waking and throughout the day

Best Time of Year to Perform Ritual:
All year, especially in the summer and winter when the air is extra dry, or in higher elevations.

Description of Ritual:

Purpose: This ritual is designed to achieve a state of pure health, mental clarity, and abundance of body, mind, and spirit, especially when paired with other rituals in this book.

Benefits: This ritual is designed to cleanse your whole body over time —from the inside out, balance hormones, clear up skin irritations, eliminate headaches, and enhance digestion. Everything we experience (whether irritating or blissful) results from how we care for our bodies.

Meaning: When we take the time to perform this daily ritual upon waking, we give ourselves an added boost and vitality to everything we set out to do. We don't need coffee or stimulants when we're fully hydrated. Each cell in our body can function as it is designed and the nutrition later in the day can be easily distributed. You are sending pure love to your organs and systems to function on a high level. Your amazing lymphatic system can cleanse your blood and remove toxins more easily.

Personalization: You can personalize this ritual by blessing your morning hydration beverage, and experimenting with fruit or vegetable infusions, such as lemon or cucumber slices. You can also enjoy your hydration ritual while taking a refreshing Epsom salt bath, or enjoying a cold plunge or cold shower, as I often do. Those habits support my body system to cleanse toxins, reduce inflammation, and encourage my nervous system to relax. Other times I have practiced my morning hydration ritual on the way to work, or paired with kayaking, yoga, biking, hiking, swimming, or daily chores around the house, yard, and garden.

Steps: Pour filtered or spring water into whatever size of container you would like to use. I have many different insulated water bottles, and also glass jars and bottles I enjoy, depending on where my day or weekend is taking me. Then add whatever flavors you have on hand from the materials listed above. Sometimes if I am gone all day or weekend, I will make myself several different types of infused water creations to last me until I return home. It is my way of supporting my body with the utmost love and care.

Share the Experience:

Throughout my twenties, thirties, and forties, I experimented with many lifestyles, including the ever-marketed caffeine and soda industries, and party culture. This was destined to show me the way to balance and wellness—or take me down. At an early age, I decided not to become addicted to caffeine, alcohol, or nicotine, and every imbalance I suffered, or witnessed in others, brought me closer to achieving my goals. Other non-health-minded cultures showed me that living in balance is preferred over anxiety and constant turmoil in my body and life. There's no doubt that experience is the greatest teacher.

In my mid-forties I joined the wellness revolution by becoming a licensed massage therapist, microcurrent practitioner, and health coach. I wanted to support others in their journey to wellness but, to succeed in helping others, first I had to be in top physical and mental health. Being my best would give me the energy to fulfill my desires and wishes.

Setting wellness intentions has always started with taking clear actions upon waking, but a good night's rest is also important. Throughout the last few years, I have seen amazing results with my deliberate hydration rituals that have come after learning to listen to my body's need for deep and restful sleep. Setting clear boundaries for myself has taken a lifetime to assimilate. No amount of hydration could help me when I was drowning in toxins and sleep deprivation as a result of an all-nighter caring for my young children, or partying with friends or my military husband. My overall health was always regained through wisdom from wise ancestors and my mindful hydration ritual.

Time and time again, I have come back to this ancient ritual. It has given me a sturdy foundation to springboard into many other avenues of hydration, including my next adventure: becoming a certified Watsu Therapist. Water Shiatsu (Watsu) is a one-on-one session in which a therapist gently cradles, moves, stretches, and massages a receiver in chest-deep warm water. Hydration has been foundational for maximum benefit for everything I offer, including microcurrent rapid recovery for fascia and scar pain, plus stem cell/copper peptide activating patches. Achieving wellness for myself and assisting others in this way is my life and passion.

Reflect on the Impact:

The impact of my mindful hydration ritual has been sustainable health with no need for medications, no new teeth cavities in adulthood, strong bone health, and flexible movement. It has enabled me to embrace a satisfying career, and life, and plenty of energy to do everything I enjoy, especially dancing and moving my body in healthy ways. Over the years, my life has unfolded in profound ways as a result of listening to and reading wellness advocate advice—and not following the crowd. Being surrounded by other mindful hydration experts and enthusiasts has been fulfilling and life-affirming. May you be guided to find your unique healing journey, and enjoy lifelong wellness with mindful hydration at the helm.

Dehydration can lead to serious complications including:

• *Heat injury:* If you don't drink enough fluids when you're exercising vigorously and perspiring heavily, you may end up with a heat injury that can range in severity from mild heat cramps to heat exhaustion or potentially life-threatening heatstroke.

• *Urinary and kidney problems:* Prolonged or repeated bouts of dehydration can cause urinary tract infections, kidney stones, and even kidney failure.

• *Seizures:* Electrolytes—such as potassium and sodium—help carry electrical signals from cell to cell. If your electrolytes are out of balance, the normal electrical messages can become mixed up, which can lead to involuntary muscle contractions, and sometimes a loss of consciousness.

• *Low blood volume shock (hypovolemic shock):* This is one of the most serious, and sometimes life-threatening, complications of dehydration. It occurs when low blood volume causes a drop in blood pressure and a drop in the amount of oxygen in your body.

Prevention:

To prevent dehydration, drink plenty of fluids and eat foods high in water, such as fruits and vegetables. Letting thirst be your guide is an adequate daily guideline for most healthy people.

People may need to take in more fluids if they are experiencing conditions such as:

• *Vomiting or diarrhea:* If your child is vomiting or has diarrhea, start giving extra water or an oral rehydration solution at the first signs of illness. Don't wait until dehydration occurs.

• *Strenuous exercise:* It's best to start hydrating the day before strenuous exercise. Producing lots of clear, dilute urine is a good indication that you're well-hydrated. During the activity, replenish fluids at regular intervals and continue drinking water or other fluids after you're finished.

• *Hot or cold weather:* You need to drink additional water in hot or humid weather to help lower your body temperature and replace what you lose through sweating. You may also need extra water in cold weather to combat moisture loss from dry air, particularly at higher altitudes

• *Illness:* Older adults most commonly become dehydrated during minor illnesses, such as influenza, bronchitis, or bladder infections. Make sure to drink extra fluids when you're not feeling well.

Water is essential to life, and helps the body by:

• Assisting regulation of normal body temperature

• Lubricating and cushioning joints

• Protecting spinal cord and sensitive tissues

• Providing a medium for metabolic and neurotransmitter activity

• Eliminating waste (urination, perspiration, bowel movements, and breathing)

• Forming saliva and mucus to maintain tissue membranes

• Making minerals and nutrients accessible to cells and tissues

• Preventing kidney stones and damage

• Reducing the chance/severity of hangovers

> *Hydration Blessings to you all!*
> *The Earth is my home*
> *All children of the Earth are my brothers and sisters*
> *Water cleanses and nourishes the Earth*
> *Water cleanses the blood of my body*
> *My body is what animates my life*

My body is mostly made of water

My eyes are dry and sting when I am dehydrated

When my internal sea is parched, I burn with anger, depression, and sadness

When my body is satisfied, it shines like the sun

When I shine like the sun, I am a beacon of hope for all who desire wellness

Let's share the love of Earth's healing waters every day!

—Heather Livesay Brown

Follow the QR code For MINDFUL HYDRATION FOR YOUR BODY,MIND, AND SOUL

About the Author

HEATHER LIVESAY BROWN

Heather Livesay Brown is a dedicated licensed massage therapist, who is currently lending her healing touch at a doctor and nurse-led hospital in S.E. Iowa. With a deep passion for holistic wellness, Heather is also an advanced Frequency Specific Microcurrent practitioner and Holistic Health Coach from the Institute of Integrative Nutrition. Her journey in health and wellness reflects her autodidactic nature, as she constantly seeks to expand her knowledge and skills.

Beyond her professional pursuits, Heather finds immense joy in her roles as a wife to Michael and a mother to her two grown sons, as well as Macy, as their cherished tabby cat. Her approach to life is guided by the principle of balance, embracing healthy living while indulging in occasional fun, following the 80/20 rule with gusto.

Heather's journey has been one of diverse experiences. Before her immersion in health and wellness, she embarked on an adventurous path as the spouse of an Iraq War veteran and as a full-time home-schooling mom, navigating the joys and challenges of unconventional education with creativity and passion.

In all aspects of her life, Heather exemplifies a commitment to holistic well-being, a thirst for knowledge and adequate hydration, and a spirit of adventure that enriches both her personal and professional endeavors.

In her spare time, Heather enjoys biking, kayaking, and traveling.

Connect with Heather:

- **Website**: www.heatherleighbrown.massagetherapy.com
- **Facebook:** facebook.com/heather.l.brown.908

The Sacred Wound

REVEALING HIDDEN TRUTHS OF THE SOUL

TEN YEARS AGO, I was experiencing overwhelming feelings of sadness and despair. I felt lonely and struggled with a lot of pain and suffering around feelings of abandonment and low self-worth. Many times, I had questioned if I was truly lovable and capable of keeping love in my life. Those limiting beliefs and deeply ingrained programs prevented me from moving forward, feeling love, and reaching my goals in more ways than I can describe. They left me feeling stuck in a life that delivered little joy or abundance—until I discovered a pathway that promised to help me break free, again and again. With an open mind, I decided to go deeper to find the healing I longed for.

One afternoon I sat on my living room floor and lit a candle as soft music played in the background. With a pen, I drew a circle in the middle of the paper, contemplated the driving force behind my feelings, and wrote, "I am not enough." In those first four steps, I gained a deeper appreciation for my life through journaling, openly releasing my pain, and setting new, positive intentions. The renewed perspective transformed my inner belief system from overwhelming grief to joy for my blessings and the future I designed for myself.

At step five, I closed my eyes in meditation. I laid a hand over my heart, marking the first time I intentionally placed a hand on myself in a healing manner. I said, "I am enough," and as my body swayed to the music, my emotions poured forth in a powerful but remarkably soothing way. Warmth enveloped my whole being as I fell into "Child's Pose," pulling my legs close to my body for a few moments before releasing them. As I did this tears flowed freely over my cheeks. My body movements and sensations felt natural and intuitive as I accepted abundant love and support from my divine self and from the universe. Somehow, I knew everything would be okay in that emotionally raw, but beautiful, moment.

Since that initial experience, I have gained clarity around many negative thoughts or behavior patterns, such as emotional eating, fears of not being safe, low self-esteem, a lack of confidence, or diminished self-worth. Admittedly, I do not always execute the process in the same way. Sometimes, I use only the meditation step; other times, I diligently walk through all six steps, journaling throughout the process. How I execute the ritual depends on what I need at the moment, and how much time and space I have available to me.

The more I perform this process, the better results I get; it's as though each time builds on the last. As I weed out the blocks in my thinking, the stagnant and painful energy is released, creating space to set a positive, empowering intention to experience and meditate on. As in the first time, I continue to experience physical reactions: overwhelming sensations of warmth, feelings of being hugged by my higher self or universal love, electrical sensations pulsating up and down my body, or waves of emotions washing over me. By the end, I walk away with a sense of relief, free from the heaviness I felt, and also feeling intuitively divine, as if completely self-supported to achieve anything I desire. The practice has proven, and continues to prove, that connecting with emotional and psychic energies delivers my most incredible, enlightening, "Ah-ha!" moments of love and support.

In the past, when I couldn't work through my stumbling blocks using pure intellect or classic problem-solving techniques, I would become far more frustrated and wind up further from my desired outcome. I couldn't disconnect from the harmful things I was feeling or believing about myself. Yet when I allowed myself to close off the world and open the floodgates of my heart space to flow freely, I was able to let go of the roots of my pain and, oftentimes, pull them out of the ground for good. With extreme clarity of thought, energies passed through me, allowing such incredible experiences as deceased loved ones coming through and presenting themselves to me. My experiences with this ritual have blessed me with a deeper connection to my higher self, a sacred space to release my pain and suffering, and the capacity to better understand who I am at my core.

If I am to define the best, or most significant, gift of this practice, it is that I can revisit these steps whenever and wherever I want, while being confident about their effectiveness in my life. I've never had a time when it didn't yield something positive, teach me more about myself, or provide much-needed guidance that I didn't know I needed.

The best advice I can give you is to go through all the steps as described, put aside all distractions, and be as open as you can to receive exactly what you need—keeping in mind that, sometimes, it is different than you may think.

The Ritual: Revealing the Truths of the Soul

This ritual asks you to explore the most profound wounds or "stuck" points in your life, so you can experience profound breakthroughs and healing. Such a transformative ritual can provide you with awareness, forgiveness, acceptance, healing, growth, abundance, and spiritual awakening—creating a stronger connection between your body, mind, spirit, and soul.

You will need a pad of paper or journal, along with a pencil or pen, music, candles (if preferred), and a sacred place or space. The steps are designed to take anywhere from 45 to 60 minutes. You can perform them whenever and wherever works best for you. To truly benefit from this ritual, however, you must be able to block out any distractions—create quiet quality time for yourself.

This ritual aims to bring awareness, growth, expansion, empowerment, and light to the most challenging, or what I refer to as "stuck," areas of your life. Stuck areas are those fixed thoughts, patterns, or actions that keep you from moving forward and living your best life as your most engaged self. The detailed actions will show you how to shift your focus toward emotional well-being and enable that deep inner cleansing to foster personal growth, connection, and transformation previously halted by your limiting self-beliefs or your unconscious patterns and behaviors. I promise you that by giving yourself this gift, you will finally reveal your truths and start on a journey toward healing.

Let's get started.

Gather the suggested materials and find your sacred space and time. Ensure that all distractions are quieted so you can devote this time to yourself. Each step will use its sheet of paper. Title each one after the steps below to easily identify the progression and order.

STEP I: THE SACRED WOUND - "AWARENESS" (3 TO 5 MINUTES)

On the first sheet of paper, draw a circle, leaving ample room around it. In the middle of the circle, write down the limiting belief and or painful event that is causing you suffering—be it physical, emotional, or mental.

Then, draw lines out from the circle, resembling a sun or flower.

On each line, write out examples as to why you believe this stuck point is happening to you. For example, if your stuck point for this session is *"I never get a good night's sleep,"* then examples of why this may be happening could include:

• *My mind races at night and I can not shut it off.*

• *My belief is that not sleeping well is a normal part of aging.*

• *My struggle with unresolved worry and anxiety about my past, uncertainty about my future, or underlying health issues.*

• *My need to go to the bathroom two-to-four times per night.*

• *My need to watch TV or use my phone while lying in bed.*

STEP II: THE SACRED WOUND - "THE RIPPLE EFFECT" (3 TO 5 MINUTES)

In this step, you will uncover how your stuck point is negatively impacting your behaviors and your everyday function in life. For example, with a stuck point of *"I never get a good night's sleep,"* possible ways this affects you could include:

• *I feel agitated most of the time.*

• *My mind is foggy and sluggish throughout the day.*

• *It is hard for me to focus and concentrate.*

• *I feel more emotionally sensitive than normal.*

• *My health and well-being suffer.*

STEP III: THE SACRED WOUND - "FINDING ANSWERS" (3 TO 5 MINUTES)

In this step, you will discover ways in which you can find possible solutions to your stuck point. For example, for a stuck point of *"I never get a good night's sleep,"* possible solutions could include:

• *I will rule out any potential health abnormalities or concerns.*

• I will experiment by shutting the TV off at night before I go to bed.

• I will commit to meditating or doing deep breathing exercises for five-to-ten minutes before bed to give my body a chance to unwind and relax.

• I will research natural sleeping aids or supplements to help me get a deeper sleep.

• I will monitor how much fluid I consume before bedtime.

STEP IV: THE SACRED WOUND - "SETTING THE INTENTION" (3 TO 5 MINUTES)

Like in Step I, draw a large circle.

Ask yourself: What do I want to feel or experience that is the opposite of what I am going through? For example, if your stuck point is *"I never get a good night's sleep,"* then in the center of the circle you could write: *I sleep soundly throughout the night.*

Imagine for a moment that your intention is your new reality. If that were the case, then what would someone who sleeps soundly throughout the night feel like or experience because of this shift? For example:

• I feel energized throughout the day.

• I feel well-rested.

• I can focus and concentrate on anything that needs my attention.

• "My emotional state of mind is balanced and centered.

STEP V: THE SACRED WOUND - "THE MEDITATION" (10-30 MINUTES)

The meditation will take the most time. Sit, stand, or lay down, whichever helps you relax and remain present.

Use your breath to create a connection with your physical, emotional, and spiritual body—deep inhales through the nose and long, slow exhales through the mouth, making sighing noises if desired. Get in tune with your breathing and feel the peace and calm envelop you. Note: you can add music or sound frequency to your meditation if this feels right.

When you are ready, place your hands on the part of your body that you feel needs the most love, attention, and support—such as your heart, belly, throat, legs, etc. State your intention, as defined in Step IV, out loud or in your mind. With each exhale feel the stuck point (Step I) leaving your body. With each inhale, feel your intention set forth, illuminating your soul.

Allow your body to move as you feel called, and signify when you have fully replaced your pain with a new, empowering belief or intention. The beauty of this meditation lies in that it allows you to get out of your headspace and into your heart. As you come to a place of stillness and surrender, know that it is safe to give up the struggle, to trust that you will find the answers you need, and that you are being divinely guided and supported.

STEP VI: THE SACRED WOUND: "THE EVOLUTION" (5 MINUTES)

Use this time to reflect on the prior steps and this ritual. List all the emotions, thoughts, experiences, breakthroughs, or revelations that you experienced during this time. Journaling this process will allow you to revisit and remind yourself what you learned—you have an incredible tool at your disposal.

Final Thoughts

The beauty of this ritual is that it can be done wherever and whenever it suits you. You need nothing more than to find your sacred space and channel your thoughts to move away from the beliefs holding you back and move to more empowering perceptions that support you in living as your higher self. I use this ritual all the time, and it has transformed my connection with my inner self and delivered me to a happier existence, allowing me to reach greater success than I could have had without it.

First, I encourage you to practice how I instructed and allow it to become an ingrained, go-to self-healing tool. Then, you can tailor the steps and timing to fit your needs whenever the mood strikes you. For example, if your time is less than suggested, adjust the steps accordingly, maybe eliminating the writing. Simply follow the steps using your mind, or even shorten the meditation period. As with all of the rituals, books, and oracle cards that I offer, I want people to have the freedom and flexibility to make things work according to their personal and professional needs at each given moment. Adaptability is key to generating the most impactful results in self-transformative work. I wish you an abundance of goodness and light in your life!

Remember, you are doing this for yourself. There is no judgment on what you put down on those papers. Your responses are for your personal use only, so to receive the maximum benefit, be as clear, honest, and real as possible, and accept the universe's gifts that may be bestowed upon you. And when you feel you may be reverting to negative thoughts or behaviors again, journal every moment and revisit what you experienced.

Approach this process with respect, afford yourself kindness and grace as you work through the steps and, in the end, embrace the amazing energy and love of who you are and what you receive. My wish for you is that you come to see the beauty inside yourself that has been there all along!

Follow the QR code to be guided through the
"I AM" MEDITATION

About the Author

JANNA LEMUR

Janna Lemur is a Motivational Speaker, Healthcare Advocate, Registered Nurse, and Military Veteran who is dedicated to helping humanity transform their trauma into triumph and pain into power.

In her roles as a Speaker, Author, and Spiritual Intuitive, Janna has committed her life to empowering military veterans, healthcare workers, students, and corporations by sharing her distinctive fusion of wisdom, insight, and practical tools to provide healing, growth, and breakthroughs.

Janna's motivational journey reflects an unwavering dedication to personal growth, resilience, and purpose. Her talks resonate deeply, instilling inspiration to embrace strength, cultivate resilience, and unlock innate potential.

In her capacity as a Spiritual Intuitive, Janna also conducts personalized corporate sessions, where she guides individuals and groups on a spiritual journey towards wholeness, while emphasizing the importance of inner peace and growth.

Available for engagements, workshops, and collaborations, Janna aims to bring inspiration and empowerment to diverse audiences, leaving a lasting positive impact.

Embark on a transformative journey with Janna Lemur as she catalyzes change, inspires resilience, and empowers individuals to unlock their fullest potential.

Connect with Janna:
www.jannalemur.com
Info@jannalemur.com

Harnessing Unlimited Potential

A NEW MOON RITUAL FOR ALIGNING YOUR ACTIONS WITH YOUR DEEPEST DESIRES

WHAT TO EXPECT from the Ritual/Practice:

This ritual will help you harness the unlimited potential available in the energy of the New Moon. It isn't just about going through the motions or "wishing on a star," so to speak; it is a tangible tool to connect you with desires you may not yet be able to articulate.

Materials/Supplies Needed:

• Quiet, comfortable, uninterrupted space to practice the ritual

• Internet access, a device to listen on, and headphones (*optional*)

• Journal, notebook, sketchbook, voice notes app, or another way to document your received insights

The ritual is accompanied by a Soul Wisdom Journey, which functions similarly to a guided meditation. It is a journey into your inner landscape to connect with, and receive, guidance from your soul's wisdom. This particular ritual and Soul Wisdom Journey is most potent when used during a New Moon to help you determine your most aligned next steps. Listen to the Soul Wisdom Journey audio included in this chapter to receive guidance from your soul wisdom.

Optimal Time of Day to Perform the Ritual:

The optimal time of day to perform this ritual is in the early morning —just before, or around the same time as, the Sun rises for the day. The Moon is often associated with the night sky, yet it is always present, as is the Sun. Our ability to see each is affected by the presence of the other. When compared to the seasons you know in nature, the New Moon is most like Spring energy, and is most potent in the first quarter of the day (midnight to six am).

Follow the QR code the Soul Wisdom Journey

Description of the Ritual:

1. Purpose: This ritual will help you tap into your inner wisdom and align your actions with your true desires and intentions. It is a powerful tool to gain clarity and insight, especially during times of transition or when faced with important decisions to make. It is also a fantastic tool to engage regularly as a devotional practice to connect with your intuitive guidance and maintain alignment with your big-picture desires.

2. Benefits: Through this ritual, you can expect to gain a clearer sense of direction and purpose that will radiate out into all areas of your life, business, and relationships.

In your business, it can:

• Illuminate the steps you need to take to reach your goals

• Ignite your creativity and intuition

• Inspire new ideas or approaches to challenges

In your relationships, it can:

• Deepen your connection with others

• Enhance your ability to communicate

• Set exquisite boundaries, leading to healthier and more satisfying interactions

This is just the beginning. The more regularly you engage it at the beginning of a new Moon cycle, the more attuned you become to the energetic flow that is always supporting your most expansive and prosperous evolution.

3. Symbolism or Meaning: The Moon holds deep symbolic significance in many cultures and spiritual traditions. It is often associated with Divine Feminine energy, intuition, and the subconscious mind. As the Moon waxes and wanes, it symbolizes the cycles of life, growth, and transformation.

The different phases of the Moon carry their own symbolism.

• The New Moon represents new beginnings; it is a time for setting intentions and planting seeds for the future.

• As the Moon waxes, it symbolizes growth, expansion, and the manifestation of those intentions.

• The Full Moon, with its bright and luminous presence, is often seen as a time of culmination, fulfillment, and abundance, and is a time to reflect on how far you've come within the journey of this cycle.

• Finally, as the Moon wanes, it represents release, integration, and surrendering to the natural cycles of life.

Astrologically speaking, your Moon placement represents the lens through which you understand yourself. It is how you most naturally receive the insights available through your lived experiences and the format or realm through which they are most potent and accessible.

4. Personalization: You can use this ritual any time you wish to tap into your inner guidance as you begin something new. The first six hours of each day is the most potent time to work with the energy of the New Moon phase. It is possible to tap into its supportive guidance during other phases, as needed, but it will be most vibrant during the New Moon.

Make this ritual your own. If you work with Tarot or Oracle cards, you could begin or end your practice with an anchor card. You may prefer to begin/end your practice with a prayer or mantra if that is something you generally incorporate. You'll notice that there are several options listed for how to document the insights you receive. If you are someone who processes through movement, you may prefer to take this whole practice on a walk instead of being inside and sitting still. There are so many ways to personalize it to fit your preferences!

5. Process:

1. Prepare Your Sacred Space: Find a quiet and comfortable space where you can immerse yourself fully in this transformative experience. To create a relaxing environment and start engaging your sensory mind, you can:

• Light a candle

• Burn incense

• Dab a few drops of your favorite essential oil on your palms, rub them together, and hold them near your face for a few breaths

This will help you disconnect from your daily responsibilities and fully honor this moment as a sacred ritual of self-discovery and alignment.

2. Connect with Your Intentions: Take a few deep breaths to center yourself and connect with your innermost desires and aspirations. As you do this, visualize your goals and intentions shimmering brightly in the dark sky, like stars guiding your way forward. Feel the energy of the New Moon amplify your intentions and infuse them with renewed purpose and clarity.

3. Embark on the Soul Wisdom Journey: Now, close your eyes and listen to the Soul Wisdom Journey provided for you. Let the soothing voice guide you through the wise landscape in your inner world, where unseen truths and insights abound.

Allow yourself to be fully present in this moment, open to receiving whatever messages the universe has to offer, knowing that they do not need to make sense in your logical mind for them to be useful.

4. Reflect on Your Insights: As the journey ends, gently open your eyes and return to the present moment. Take a few moments to reflect on the insights you've gained. You may choose to record your thoughts and feelings in a journal, capture them in a voice note, or express them through a creative practice such as drawing or intuitive movement.

5. Fortify the Flow: This ritual is a powerful tool to align your actions with your true purpose and intentions. It invites you to step into the flow of the universe, where synchronicities abound and opportunities unfold effortlessly.

Embrace the potential of what this practice will bring with an open heart and a willingness to change, knowing you are guided and supported every step of the way. Understand that you can return to the wisdom of your journey at any time, by connecting with your breath and asking for additional guidance.

6. Step Forward with Clarity: As you continue on your journey, take note of how the Moon continues to support you throughout all the phases of this Lunar Cycle. May the wisdom and guidance you've received through this ritual lead you toward embodying your deepest desires and aspirations.

My Experience with the Ritual:

I've always been drawn to the Moon. Like so many people, my relationship with the Moon began as a curiosity and spark of joy lit up in the night sky, our connection generally perceived as happenstance.

Over the years, our relationship has deepened and become more intentional.

Astrology and tracking Moon phases have been amazing tools in all areas of my life, especially my business. Through regular engagement, I have noticed profound shifts in my creative flow, become more in tune with my inner voice and natural cycles, and learned to trust the process that is unique for me.

One of the most significant changes I've experienced is my approach to working with my long-term goals. By setting intentions at each New Moon and taking small, consistent actions throughout the Lunar Cycle, I've seen remarkable progress in my business. I no longer feel overwhelmed by big-picture projects because I know I can work through them in a digestible and playful way. Understanding the energetics of each Lunar phase has been so nourishing for my nervous system and puts my mind at ease. I know there are certain times meant for dreaming, others designed for building, periods for reflection, and even a time when the most important action I can take is to rest.

I've noticed these to be true for my clients as well. While there is an underlying focus on the full cycle of development that occurs annually in our work together, we use the Moon as a guide to help bring attention to the smaller cycles that live within each larger one. I work primarily with multi-passionate visionaries and creators who are creating a big impact through their work. It can be quite easy for these individuals to be so engrossed in the big picture of their creation that the day-to-day feels overwhelming. Working with the Moon cycles helps ground in the work they are doing in a supportive and tangible way.

When I first started using the Moon cycles as a way of keeping time in my business, I began by checking in only at the New and Full Moon phases. This was beautifully supportive as it gave me a regular rhythm of tuning in to where I was, and consciously realigning with my desired destination. Over time, as I developed my body of work around the personal seasons, I realized that the Moon cycles also contain seasons, and that each season provides something unique to support us as we move within it.

Working with the Moon cycle can go so much deeper than just setting intentions at the New Moon and checking in about what to release at the Full Moon. And it also doesn't have to. My best advice to you is to be where you are. Allow this relationship to unfurl in organic timing and don't try to force it. However, if you are feeling the call to develop this further and have found benefit in the ritual provided in this chapter, I invite you to explore how we may work together on that journey.

About the Author

REGYNA CURTIS

Regyna Curtis is a game-changer in the world of entrepreneurship. Her breakthrough approach, "Charting Your Course," empowers business owners to align their business with their unique energy using astrology and intuitive insight. As the visionary founder of Atmaitri, Regyna is renowned for unlocking individuals' unlimited potential, especially during the powerful New Moon phase. Her chapter features a transformative ritual that will guide readers in identifying and achieving their most dynamic goals throughout the lunar cycle.

Regyna's wealth of experience has earned her international best-seller status, with published works spanning spirituality, entrepreneurship, and intuition development. Her expertise has been showcased on popular podcasts, blogs, articles, and television features. Through her signature seasonal retreats, Regyna seamlessly integrates self-care practices with entrepreneurial wisdom, offering a holistic approach to personal and professional growth.

Connect with Regyna:
Website: http://www.atmaitri.com
Charting Your Course: https://www.atmaitri.com/charting-your-course
Instagram: https://www.instagram.com/atmaitri/

Facebook: https://www.facebook.com/regyna.curtis
LinkedIn: https://www.linkedin.com/in/regyna-curtis/

From Heartbreak To Healing

EMBRACING THE UNEXPECTED

DECEMBER 1992 WAS the first time I realised something was not right in my body. This was a mere six weeks since my heart had been wrenched out and stomped on after the sudden loss of my brother in a motorcycle accident. Upon waking, I had an irresistible urge to start scratching, and as I dressed for work, I glanced at my body to see angry red welts where I'd unconsciously scratched throughout the night. As the day progressed, so did the increased urge to scratch. It got so bad that even after three trips to the doctor, four blood tests, and five increases to the highest possible dose of prescribed antihistamines, I felt like my body was on fire; I was going insane with this itch that just would not stop.

Two months later, I was chronically sleep deprived, exhausted, and frustrated to the point where, one day at work, I had a meltdown and collapsed on the floor in a blubbering mess. Days later I was on a plane to Brisbane to visit an allergy specialist. Within minutes of conducting a RAST test he delivered another crushing blow; I was having a severe reaction to wheat. "Great," I thought, "there goes all my favourite foods, biscuits, cakes, pies, pizza and, of course, bread."

Not to mention that 1992 was years before the wheat-free, gluten-free, dairy-free world we live in today.

After a very long, drawn out fifteen months of being denied my favourite foods, I was able to reintroduce wheat into my diet, and was going on to live a "normal life." Or so I thought. I may have moved on, but my body was keeping score.

Fast forward to 2010: after travelling the world in my twenties, I was happily married with two young sons. Little did I know, but life was about to come crashing down around me—again. On a seemingly ordinary Friday night, I'd just put our kids to bed and, as I flopped down on the couch next to my husband, he turned to me and said, "I don't think I can stay married to you any longer." *What? Where did that come from? I mean, I know we have our problems, as most couples do, but I didn't think they were that bad.* He, on the other hand, had different ideas.

This conversation, as you can imagine, didn't bode well for me or my health and quickly, I skyrocketed down into a deep, dark abyss, an emotional quicksand that re-awakened my slumbering wheat allergy as well as igniting thirty-three different food intolerances that caused my weight to plummet to a dangerously low fifty-one kilograms. Throw in chronic fatigue, sleepless nights, back, neck and shoulder pain from living in a perpetual state of fight, flight, freeze—and by 2013, wallowing in self-pity, I hit an all-time new rock bottom. I turned to Red Bull energy drinks just to get through the day.

One day, my boss sat me down and said, "Leisa, do you realise you tell everyone you meet all your life's problems within five minutes of meeting you?" I was mortified; I could feel the heat rising up my neck, colouring my face with guilt, shame, and embarrassment. *Is that really the image I am projecting out into the world? Am I really playing the victim?*

As I sat there letting his words sink in, I burst into tears, overwhelmed by a feeling of utter helplessness, not knowing how I could possibly turn my life around. Suddenly, I heard a "ding" come from my computer. I glanced up and froze instantly; my divorce lawyer's name was at the top of my emails. With a ball of dread knotting in my stomach, I clicked open the email. Inside was another ten thousand dollar legal bill. What sanity I had left, flooded out of me like a levy breaking its banks.

At that moment, I decided that before the lawyers got all my money, I would book the trip to Machu Picchu I had put on my bucket list back in 2003.

Six weeks later, I was on a plane. Seven days after that, as I stood overlooking the Sacred Valley of the Incas, I prayed for a miracle to set me free of this toxic cycle I'd trapped myself in. On day nine, as I trekked through the Amazon jungle, I received confirmation that someone up there in heaven must have heard my cry.

It had poured rain overnight, and many parts of our twelve kilometre trek were blocked by knee deep water. I felt a familiar dread wash over me as I gingerly stepped out of the boat onto the soft, wet sand. My guide was already powering through the thick jungle terrain, and it was either "suck it up" or be left behind. Fear is a wonderful motivator, so I scurried along to keep up with the group. At the halfway point, we stopped for lunch. As I sat there—soaking wet, utterly exhausted—I realised I'd just trekked through one of the most treacherous jungles in the world.

Suddenly my brain screamed at me, "What do you think you're doing? Have you forgotten you have chronic fatigue?" Yes, that was true. Since my boys were born, I had lived in a perpetual cloud of brain fog, lethargy, and severe exhaustion. But in that moment, I realised that our minds can be stronger than our bodies. Then and there, I decided that when I got back home, I would take back control and reclaim my life.

I didn't know it at the time, but this statement kickstarted a profound healing and personal growth journey that would become a lifeline that kept me anchored through many more dark and stormy days.

Upon my return from Peru, two incidents stoked the embers of what little self-confidence I had. Firstly, a friend suggested I keep a gratitude journal. My response was, "What have I got to be grateful for, my life is a mess?" The second occurred when a stranger asked what I did for self-love. As I stared blankly at her, I asked, "What's that?"

Today, my life is full and rich of what I call the four selves: Self-love, Self-worth, Self-confidence, and Self-esteem. Incorporating these rituals into your life will lay the foundation to transform your life from where you are, to where you desire to be.

It is my hope and wish for all who read my story that it can be the catalyst for your own journey towards a happier, healthier, more confident you.

RITUAL 1 – GRATITUDE

Purpose:

Gratitude is like a mental vitamin, and is a powerful magnet for the Law of Attraction. Neuroscience studies show gratitude activates our brain's reward centres, which release dopamine and serotonin—neurochemicals associated with optimism, camaraderie, and positive emotions [1]

Benefits:

• **Healthier you:** Strengthen the immune system, reduce body aches and pains, improve sleep cycles.

• **Healthier relationships:** Open your heart chakra and increase empathy, foster better communication and harmonious connections with others.

• **Increased fulfilment**: Create a positive feedback loop in the brain, which leads to an enhanced sense of purpose and self-satisfaction.

---

1. Chowdhury, Madhuleena Roy. The Neuroscience of Gratitude and Effects on the Brain. PositivePsychology.com. May 02, 2024

• **Raises vibrational frequency**: Aligns us with higher energies to manifest what we desire, through deepening our spiritual connection.

Steps:

1. Upon waking, while your mind is still in an awake but relaxed (alpha brainwave) state[2], silently give thanks for at least three things you're grateful for. Allowing your mind to drift during this relaxed state enhances neuroplasticity and positively anchors emotions to those specific things. This reinforces the neural pathways associated with appreciation and abundance, shifting your mindset and setting the stage to attract more positivity into your life.

2. When you're ready to get out of bed, state something positive to yourself.

> My favourite is: "I love how excited I am to see what adventures unfold today." This sparks your deep unconscious motivation filter. [3]

3. Write down what you're grateful for. This can be done in the morning or evening; when I first started, I did it at night. As I progressed and learned I could manifest through gratitude, I began to use the morning for manifesting and the evening for what had happened throughout the day. Here are some examples:

> Morning: "I am grateful for seeing the shoes I wanted go on sale."
> Evening: "I am grateful for two new clients."

If you're new to gratitude journaling, and life is currently a bit of a mess, you may think you have nothing to be grateful for. However,

---

2. www.sciencedirect.com/topics/agricultural-and-biological-sciences/brain-waves
3. James, Dr Tad & Woodsmall, Wyatt. Time Line™ Therapy and The Basis of Personality, 1988

writing down even simple things like the sun coming out today still activates the neurochemicals needed to start shifting your reality.

RITUAL 2 – SELF-LOVE AND SELF-CARE

Purpose:

Growing up, we are not taught how vital self-love and self-care are. In fact, too often, we have limiting beliefs installed from childhood that cause us to think that if we look after number one, we will be seen as selfish, vain, or self-centred. This ritual is designed to challenge you on your thinking and break any cycles of feeling that you must put others needs before your own.

Self-love and self-care are a team, and together, they teach us how to nurture ourselves in a way that reminds us to fill our cup before we fill others.

Benefits:

• **Higher self-esteem:** A healthier acceptance of our self-image reduces internal negative brain chatter.

• **Increased motivation:** Loving ourselves helps us pursue our goals, hopes, wishes, and dreams to create a fulfilling life.

• **Strengthens our determination:** Believing in ourselves fuels our drive to achieve.

• **Enhances self-awareness:** Tuning into our needs, desires, and emotions empowers us to make informed decisions from our higher self.

• **Reduces anxiety**: Treating ourselves with compassion alleviates stress and promotes serenity within.

• **Better sleep**: Honouring our physical and emotional needs contributes to improved sleep quality, allowing the body to rest and repair.

How to:

Think about where, what, and to whom you are currently giving your energy. Is it to yourself first?

Self-love and self-care include dedicating time for yourself, and setting boundaries that honour your time, space, and energy.

Self-love can be given anywhere, anytime. The key is to establish a practice that suits you, your lifestyle, and fills you up the most. Here are five easy steps to get you started:

1. Take a piece of paper and write:

    1. What's important to you about self-love and self-care. Think about what outcome you want from this practice.

    2. Ask yourself this question again, adding to your list until you run out of things to write.

    3. Now number them in order of importance.

2. Write a list of activities that light you up and bring you joy. Keep writing until you have exhausted all activities.

3. Highlight three items on your list to incorporate into your life over the next thirty days. Be sure to select *at least one item* that can be incorporated into a daily or weekly routine.

4. Write your three items on a separate piece of paper. Make four columns titling them: *What, When, Where,* and *Outcome.* Your outcome will be a combination of what's important (from Step 1) and how it makes you feel. Complete the columns, referring to the example below:

- **What**
- **When**
- **Where**

- **Outcome**

What	When	Where	Outcome
Digging my feet in the sand at the water's edge.	After my morning walk, three times a week	The Strand Beach	Makes me feel relaxed, like all my worries are being washed out to sea
Getting my hair cut and coloured	Every six weeks	Hairdresser	Makes me feel beautiful, vibrant, and excited
Dancing to live music	At least once per month	Local pub	Takes me to my happy place which sparks my creativity

As you get comfortable with these practices, feel free to add a new self-care practice into your life.

Follow the QR code for the Healing Within: Cultivating Self-Love, Gratitude and Positive Thinking Meditation

About the Author

LEISA QUAGLIATA

LeisaQ, a Financial Adviser turned Financial Lifestylist, empowers women with self-confidence and financial security tools. Her passion lies in guiding women through life's financial labyrinth—whether this involves building their career, raising a family, or navigating post-divorce challenges.

By delving into her clients' emotional well-being, LeisaQ uses her skills and experience to illuminate paths out of darkness through the development of gratitude, self-love, and self-care practices. Her expertise is grounded in personal triumphs over adversity: an eight-year divorce battle, single-handedly raising her children, and coping with loss.

As an international bestselling co-author, captivating keynote speaker, and six-figure business founder, LeisaQ's voice resonates with everyday people seeking everyday wisdom. Her diverse educational background includes a Bachelor's Degree in Business and Financial Management, along with certifications in Coaching, Neuro Linguistic Programming, Hypnotherapy, and Time Line Therapy. Her unique talent lies in inspiring others to rewrite their narratives, challenge limiting beliefs, and embrace the human experience.

Connect with Leisa:
Website: www.leisaq.com
Email: leisa@leisaq.com

Bridging The Powers Of Heaven And Earth Within Your Body

ABIGAIL MENSAHBONSU-ULMER

THIS BEAUTIFULLY TRANSFORMATIVE ritual is dedicated to empaths, healers, and all those who actively work with energy. In a world that often feels chaotic and overwhelming, it is common to experience heightened levels of anxiety and stress. It is becoming increasingly crucial for us to seek connection and alignment with something greater than ourselves, as this is where we can find the true answers and attain peace of mind.

About the Ritual:

When I was at grad school, I developed a personal ritual that greatly benefited me during clinic sessions. With my background in Chinese medicine, I focused on acupuncture and Chinese herbal medicine when I treated patients in clinic. As I became more involved, my class-mates noticed my consistent energy and optimism, which was in contrast to the fatigue they were experiencing. They began to ask me questions, so I taught them techniques to manage their energy levels, based on their needs and whether they felt overstimulated or under-whelmed.

In response to my friends' curiosity and requests, I started a meditation group. Once a week, we gathered to practice meditation, and I shared tools beneficial in the clinic and in their personal lives. These energetic tools helped them navigate various aspects of life.

The experience profoundly impacted them, especially those who identified as empaths. They transformed from feeling drained by interactions to feeling energized and invigorated. They learned to be present without absorbing others' energy and to set healthy boundaries by recognizing what belonged to others and what belonged to themselves.

The tools I shared were transformative. We explored honoring our spiritual gifts, grounding ourselves, and connecting with the divine. We also learned to call upon our allies for assistance. These sessions were filled with joy as we delved into these practices together.

Seeing my classmates grow and succeed in the clinic was incredibly rewarding. Even now, they express gratitude for the lasting impact of those teachings, which they continue to practice. The simplicity of the ritual I taught holds immense power, and I am humbled by their appreciation.

The ritual began simply: ground into the Earth, connect with the heavens, and merge this energy in our hearts. We also visualized a bubble of light around us for protection and upliftment. Over time, I added elements intuitively, based on their needs.

One addition was to call upon spirit allies, which allowed everyone to connect with their guardian angels and spirit team and open new realms of guidance and support. We also called upon angels and Archangels aligned with our journeys and explored invoking specific frequencies through colors to enhance our energy; for example—a vibrant yellow for joy, an earthy red for energy, or an emerald green for healing. This ritual evolved with us, allowing each individual to experience personal growth and connection.

Engaging in this ritual became essential to my daily routine as it set the tone for my day or helped me cleanse and align at night. When I skipped it, I felt the difference; I felt overwhelmed by the world's struggles. When I practiced it, I remained centered, unaffected, and able to serve others better from a place of clarity and connection.

I hope that this ritual elevates your experiences as it has mine. Embrace this practice—may it bring you peace, centeredness, and clarity.

Enjoy the journey.

Materials Needed:

Essential: Your beautiful self, an open heart, and a willingness to connect with your divine team. The ritual can take anywhere from five-to-ten minutes, depending on how long you wish to engage in it.

Optional: A candle, incense, or a smudge stick (e.g., sage, palo santo).

Optimum Time to Perform This Ritual:
Morning: Performing this ritual first thing in the morning helps set a positive tone for the day.

Evening: Doing this ritual before bed cleanses any negative energy picked up during the day, promotes a restful and refreshing sleep, and sets you up for a clear morning.

Best Time to Perform the Ritual:

This ritual can be performed anywhere, at any time of the year.

Purpose of the Ritual:

The purpose of this ritual is to bridge your spiritual self with your physical self. In our current times, it is essential to integrate these two aspects. When we unite the spiritual part of who we are meant to be with our physical being, it allows us to navigate our human experience with grace. This ritual helps harmonize divinity and humanity within us.

By performing this ritual, you start your day with intention and mindfulness—which provides divine protection—and call in divine reinforcements to support you throughout the day. It transforms an ordinary day into a magical one! The ritual grounds, activates, and elevates you by blessing your day, body, mind, and heart.

Furthermore, it extends blessings to everyone you encounter. When you step into the world centered and anchored in your truth, and connected to the Divine Father and Divine Mother, those around you will also receive the benefits of your balanced and harmonious presence.

Benefits of Doing this Ritual:

Performing this ritual daily fosters a profound sense of connection. It anchors you not only to the earth but also to the divine—creating a harmonious link between heaven and earth. This sense of connection extends to those around you, purifies your day, and clears obstacles from your path. It's like having your path smoothed out, with bumps and trip hazards removed, so ensuring a more effortless journey.

The ritual also calls for divine protection which increases your sense of safety, security, and confidence as you move through the world.

Additionally, it helps you set a daily intention. Many people wake up and follow a routine on autopilot—brush their teeth, drink coffee, go to work—repeating the same actions day after day. By performing this ritual each morning, your day will become consciously intentional as you become more aware of your actions and interactions and no longer operate automatically, but with purpose and awareness.

This shift from routine to intentional living is significant. We need more individuals who are self-aware and in tune with their own energies, as well as those of the day and the people they meet. I believe this would foster greater harmony in our interactions with one another. This ritual opens you up to see and feel this heightened awareness.

Personalization:

I encourage you to practice this ritual for at least twenty-one days before making any changes as this helps establish a solid foundation. The beauty of the ritual is that it evolves with you, so you don't need to worry about rigidly following steps. As you practice, your intuition and divine communication will guide you and bring forth what you need.

Personalization happens naturally as you connect to your soul and higher self. Your soul's needs will emerge, and you will be able to incorporate those elements fluidly. The ritual is dynamic; it grows with you as you evolve and become more aligned with your true self.

One of the main advantages of this ritual is that it brings you back to yourself, fostering a deeper connection to your inner being.

The Ritual:

Find a space where you can perform this ritual without interruption.

Light your smudge stick or incense and clear your space and body.

Light your candle.

Close your eyes.

Place your hand on your heart and begin to breathe deeply.

Bring in gratitude for your breath, your body, the day, and all the blessings ready to come. Appreciate those who love and support you, your clients, your business, your mind, heart, soul, and spirit, and your divine team. Reflect on what you are grateful for.

With your hand on your heart, call your higher self into your heart and feel her presence radiate throughout your body.

From the center of your heart, envision your channel extending upward and connecting to the heart of Source (the image of the Divine or Source will be unique to you). Open yourself to receive the beautiful golden light from the Divine Father's heart into your heart. Let it flow through your body and out through your feet, creating light roots that anchor into the earth.

Now, from the center of your heart, envision your channel extending downward deep into the earth. At the center of the earth, connect to the heart of the Divine Mother and draw up her emerald green light, her divine love, nurturing, and support. Bring it up through your roots into your heart and body, and let it spread into every cell.

Return your awareness to your heart, where you have the radiance of your higher self, the golden light from the Divine Father, and the emerald green light from the Divine Mother.

See, sense, or feel all the energies converge within your heart and expand outward, creating a bubble of opalescent light around you.

Breathe into this space, connecting to above, below, and within your heart.

Take a few deep breaths.

Ask your divine team to surround you with a golden circle of light. Thank them for their love, guidance, and support.

Bring your awareness back to your heart and set an intention for the day.

• *What would you like to experience today?*

• *What experiences and miracles would you like to invite into your life?*

Set your intention and place it at the center of your heart.

Move into the quiet phase, where you listen for any messages that come in.

Ask, "What do I need to know today?" then simply listen.

Be open to receiving messages in various forms: hearing, seeing pictures, smelling, sensing, or just knowing. Spirit will communicate with you in the way you can best receive.

Once you have received what you need, close the ritual with gratitude. Say, "Thank you. Thank you. Thank you. It is done. It is done. It is done. By the power of three, a perfect Trinity, it is done."

Bring your hands together in a prayer position and bow your head slightly to close your ritual.

You are now ready for your day.

By engaging in this ritual, we reclaim our spiritual grounding and presence, which allows us to navigate the world's challenges with serenity and inner peace. Connecting to a higher power or divine presence shifts our perspective, and reminds us that we are not alone and that profound wisdom and guidance are available beyond our limitations.

This ritual helps us realign with our purpose and reconnect with our deeper selves. As empaths and healers, prioritizing self-care and nurturing is essential; this ritual is a powerful tool for ongoing personal and spiritual development.

Our purpose on Earth is to fully immerse ourselves in the human experience. Although we may feel alone at times, it is important to remember that we embarked on this journey equipped with the necessary tools and resources. These tools help us navigate life with greater meaning and purpose. While challenges will still arise, employing these tools enables us to face them with greater ease.

This ritual offers invaluable peace, divine protection, and connection. It summons the support of the divine allies who accompany us throughout the day. By practicing this ritual, we cultivate a heightened awareness of our daily experiences and how we engage with life. It opens us to receive greater divine support, magic, and blessings beyond our expectations; it transforms an ordinary day into a magical one.

Be empowered to approach each day with intention, consciousness, and an open heart, ready to receive the divine guidance and blessings abundantly available to you.

May you wholeheartedly embrace this ritual and experience its profound impact on your daily life.

May it guide you toward inner peace, clarity, and a profound connection to the divine.

Enjoy the journey and let the magic unfold.

About the Author

ABIGAIL MENSAHBONSU-ULMER

Founder of Moon Goddess Academy and Publishing, Abigail Mensah-Bonsu is a highly regarded Spiritual Guide and Mentor who is committed to elevating consciousness and embodying the divine feminine. She wears many hats as Divine Channel, Intuitive, Master Healer, internationally-acclaimed Bestselling Author and Publisher, and host of the Sovereign Goddess podcast.

Abigail empowers women to express their authentic selves and amplify their voices. She specializes in facilitating multi-author books and high-level group mentorships and programs that enable her clients to achieve greater success, impact, and resonance in their lives and endeavors.

Through compassionate yet powerful guidance, Abigail shows female Empaths, Leaders, Visionaries, and Lightworkers how to unlock their full potential, manifest abundance, and live in alignment with their highest purpose.

Themes central to Abigail's transformative work include Goddess mentorship, Feminine leadership, DNA and Light Activations, Mindset restructuring, Multidimensional healing, Archetypes, Starseeds, Awakening, and Divine remembrance.

Connect with Abigail:
Website: www.moongoddessacademy.com
Podcast: podcasters.spotify.com/pod/show/sovereigngoddess
https://linktr.ee/shaktimoongoddess

Start Your Day With GUMPTION

CONNECT TO YOUR TRUTH THROUGH MOVEMENT AND INTENTION WITH THE GUMPTION WARM-UP

WHAT TO EXPECT from the Ritual/Practice:

This moving meditation brings you into your day running on all cylinders. It takes you from tired, overwhelmed, and anxious, to energized, clear, and ready to take on what's next with a grounded, intentional presence. By the end, you'll know where and how to focus your energy and attention, honor your boundaries, and even invite more play and pleasure into your life.

Materials/Supplies Needed:

Space to move. You'll start seated on the floor and will finish standing. You will also want a journal to capture any insights brought to your awareness through the ritual.

Time Needed to Complete the Ritual:

5-8 minutes, 10-15 minutes guided

Optimal Time of Day to Perform Ritual:

At the beginning of your day or before a task that requires you to shift your focus and intention. For example: before an important meeting, or when you switch from household chores/running errands to creative projects, etc.

Best Time of Year to Perform Ritual:

It can be performed throughout the year.

Follow the QR code to be guided through the GUMPTION Warm-Up.

DESCRIPTION OF RITUAL

1. Purpose:

The GUMPTION Warm-Up is a moving meditation that taps into the innate wisdom of the body and leads to clarity, motivation, and a deep connection with yourself and your purpose. Depending on what you need each day, it will support self-care, focus, productivity, energy, and more. It recognizes the powerful dialogue between the mind and body and brings play, curiosity, and intention into that relationship.

2. Benefits:

• Activates your energy for peak emotional, mental, physical, and spiritual performance

• Shifts your state from anxious and overwhelmed to grounded, calm, and focused

• Brings clarity to deeper truths you might not be consciously aware of about a situation or project

• Builds self-trust

• Connects you with your body so that you notice when things feel good or when something is off

• Builds confidence in, and intention to, your life's direction

3. Symbolism or Meaning:

According to the Cambridge Dictionary, the definition of gumption is as follows:

"gumption (n): the ability to decide what is the best thing to do in a particular situation, and to do it with energy and determination"

The word "gumption" first came to Kerri Van Kirk, the creator of the GUMPTION Warm-up, in 2012 when she was about to start DIY touring her first album as a singer-songwriter. This was shortly after she'd lost her voice and was unable to sing, and sometimes speak, without pain. She knew she'd need gumption to get through the tour. But she also knew gumption was an acronym for something. In 2015, she wrote a poem, "When I Have Gumption," to give herself, and other women, hope and empowerment. Then in 2017, she realized the GUMPTION acronym was connected to embodiment and aligned with the chakra system. She realized that this alignment was "the natural flow of a powerful, creative vessel."

4. Personalization:

The starred elements are the classic warm-up. However, this warm-up is very flexible and intended for you to connect with the wisdom in your body.

The movement pieces can be taken out so that it becomes a seated meditation focused on the MIND aspects of the Classic Warm-Up. If you can't sit on the floor, you can start the warm-up seated in a chair, allowing any movement to focus in the torso and arms. You can allow the movement to carry you from the chair to your feet if you choose.

You can choose to play music.

It can also be used as a framework for journaling around a situation.

5. Steps or Process:

First of all, there is no right or wrong way to perform this ritual; it is a personal journey. However, to get the most out of it, allow yourself to follow what feels "right" in your body. Some days you will find yourself focused on how the movement feels. Other days, answers to the questions associated with each letter will drop in seemingly out of nowhere. Many times you will likely experience some of both.

If you feel yourself forcing your body to move in a certain way, or mentally trying to figure out an answer to one of the questions, explore how you can allow your body to move in a way that feels easy, and release your mind from needing an answer. For example, your body may be craving slower, more gentle movements if it doesn't feel good when you try to move more quickly. Allow yourself to trust those feelings, even if you are unsure of them as this will help grow your self-trust.

In the beginning, feel free to do this ritual with your eyes open or closed. I often close my eyes for the elements of the warm-up that are more still, but open them when I'm moving because I lose my balance easily. Follow what feels good to you.

Note: Allow the building energy of the Up section to bring you up to your feet if that feels good.

The GUMPTION Warm-Up

CONNECT TO YOUR TRUTH THROUGH MOVEMENT & INTENTION

Created by Kerri Van Kirk

	MIND	BODY
GROUNDED	Getting present. Who am I and what am I doing today?	*Sitting in easy pose. *Feeling energy at the base of you. Foot massage.
UP	Getting energized. How is this bringing me into the next best version of myself? What's worth getting up for?	*Circling pelvis *Gently tapping all over body Taking a walk
MUSCLE	Connecting to strength. What skills, support and resources am I bringing into my day?	*Connecting to core muscles. *Doing 10 squats. Arm dips or push ups.
PLAY/ LEASURE	Connecting to joy, heart & bringing a sense of play and pleasure into my day?	*Putting hand on heart. *Swaying/dancing/jumping Self-massage.
TRUTH	Connecting to truth. What is my truth today? Is there anything I need to say?	*Stillness, connecting to throat Speaking out loud. Journaling.
INSPIRATION	Getting inspired. What about my day inspires me? How will I inspire others today?	*Three deep breaths, while raising and lowering arms. Breath of fire.
OM	Connecting to the universe. How can today contribute to the world I want to see?	*Three Om's. Chanting/singing. Visualization.
NOW	Feeling activation through all chakras. Is there anything else I need? What's my next step?	*Tracing hands up body, into the air and down sides 3x. *Moving from presence.

Share the Experience:

Spring 2020. Things were intense. My husband, Greg, and I sold our home in December 2019 to travel with his work, not knowing what was coming three months later.

So there we were, back sharing my parents' house with my eight- and ten-year-old nieces. Initially, my sister and brother-in-law were working outside the home and, when we didn't know much about Covid-19, it felt safer for the girls to stay with us rather than passing them back and forth. While many were navigating isolation, I was caught between loving the time spent with family—playing board games, doing puzzles, and going out for bike rides—and the frustration of not having a space to be alone.

This was the perfect time for me to take a step back from my work as a functional health coach because it no longer felt aligned; focusing on my nieces and what they needed was a good excuse to let that go. But I was also feeling anxious not knowing what was next for me. In the online communities where I hung out everybody was "pivoting" their businesses, but I wasn't sure where I wanted to go next. And with all the collective fear swirling around me, I struggled to focus well enough to get clarity.

So when Kerri Van Kirk started a Facebook group to lead weekly energy healing sessions and morning GUMPTION Warm-Ups to create greater focus and intention to our days that seemed to all blend into each other, I was in. I knew I could carve out fifteen minutes for myself, even if it meant throwing in my earbuds and doing the warm-up in the middle of the living room because Greg was working out of our bedroom.

At first, I had no idea what to expect. I'd tried meditation before, but I was convinced I couldn't do it. I struggled to sit still, the voice in my head ran constantly, and I didn't know how to do it "right." But about a year or so before, I'd had an experience with a moving meditation during a moon ceremony where something inside told me to let go of my fear of being seen and judged and follow the guided instructions. Letting go and being present in the practice was a transformational experience, so I figured I'd give it another try.

At first, I was really uncomfortable. Even though only family members were in the house, I worried about who was watching me as they came down the stairs and past the living room on the way to the kitchen. I was already the "weird" one in the family, with my niece referring to me as a full witch after a tour in Salem, MA, for using essential oils and having crystals.

In the beginning, I followed Kerri's lead. I watched and copied her movements, unsure of the right way to listen to my body in this context, even though, as a physical therapist, I'd been guiding others to listen to theirs for years. But at the end of each warm-up, I felt less anxious. I'd gain an insight into what I wanted, how I was feeling, or where to focus my energy and attention that day.

This ritual became a non-negotiable part of my day as I continued this practice four days per week for about six months. Over time, I became more comfortable in trusting my instincts about what I needed, how my body wanted to move, and what clarity and insights I was bringing away from the practice.

We started this practice in mid-April, and by early June I knew exactly where I was heading. I'd come to understand that what I loved about my prior work as a physical therapist and health coach was building relationships with my patients and clients, and hearing the stories that uncovered the stressors showing up as pain and disease in their bodies. But I'd learned that focusing on the physical was only going to get them so far because we weren't addressing what was going on beneath the surface. For them to achieve true well-being, I had to look at them as a whole person.

As a physical therapist, I'd always seen myself as a mechanic for the body. Now I knew I needed to become a mechanic for the whole person. And that involved bringing new tools to my toolbox. On my self-discovery and wellness journey, I came across and played with a variety of tools. But the one that stuck with me was Human Design, and more specifically, Karen Curry Parker's Quantum Human Design™.

Quantum Human Design™ teaches us that our decisions are meant to be made based on how things feel, not whether or not we have logically figured them out. The further we went with Kerri's GUMPTION Warm-Ups while I studied QHD, the more I was able to identify these feelings in my body, and the more I was able to tell when a decision was a "yes" or a "no" based on what I was feeling in my body, not what I could rationalize in my mind. And my self-trust continued to grow.

I knew that if I was going to help my clients learn to deepen their connection with their Authentic Selves by embodying their Human Design, they would need help to tune into the messages their bodies were sending them—and I would need a tool to help them reconnect with their bodies. So I asked Kerri to train me in how to lead the GUMPTION Warm-Up so my clients could also benefit from this ritual. I've now shared the GUMPTION process as a warm-up or journaling exercise with hundreds of individuals across many walks of life, and they've all uncovered profound insights they weren't previously aware of while allowing themselves to play and connect with greater joy in the process. The GUMPTION Method reminds us we don't have to be so serious to build self-trust and strengthen our connection with, and the expression of, our Authentic Selves. Enjoy the exploration!

About the Author

KRISTEN TOSCANO

During her twenty-year career as a physical therapist, Kristen Toscano realized that, by focusing solely on relieving physical symptoms, we were missing a big piece of what the body was trying to communicate through pain. Now, as a GUMPTION Method Facilitator, certified Quantum Human Design™ Specialist, and Quantum Alignment Practitioner, she guides others on their journey of self-discovery and empowerment.

Kristen encourages her clients to live more intentionally by connecting to the innate wisdom of the body, making decisions from a place of inner knowing, trusting their intuition, and leveraging their natural gifts and talents.

Kristen has contributed to the book *Mystics Revealed: Unconventional Success Stories from Extraordinary Leaders* and has presented workshops for various organizations, including the Dog Tag Fellowship Program, where she shares her insights on Human Design, the GUMPTION Method, and intentional living.

With a passion for travel, and food and wine pairings, Kristen and her husband, Greg, have traveled to wineries across five continents.

Connect with Kristen at https://kristentoscano.com or on LinkedIn or Instagram @kristentoscano

Beyond Balance

THE ART OF LIVING INTENTIONALLY USING THE WIND DOWN METHOD

WHAT TO EXPECT from the Ritual/Practice:

In the following pages, I encourage you to embrace the art of living intentionally; to fill your life with the things that lift you, bring you joy, and allow you to shine as the brilliant individual you are. To live intentionally is to embrace the power that is yours in deciding how you spend your time. So much of our life is spent at the pull and needs of others. Unfortunately, this has left many of us feeling off balance and running on empty. This chapter is an invitation to pull at the threads of that fabric and unweave the pieces that don't serve your inner well-being.

Imagine what it could feel like to no longer be at the mercy of the demands of your life, and to navigate them with serene determination. To embrace growth opportunities and diligently deliver your work, while filling your cup with self-care and quality time with the people you love. To live intentionally is to reclaim your power and forge a sanctuary of authenticity amidst the noise of the world around us.

We will begin this process by connecting back to you. By exploring what it is to be you—without the expectations of others. Take this time to pause and consider the people and opportunities that light you up, and audit your daily activities and commitments.

Next, we will create a weekly habit to reinforce how our time is used. The weekly Wind Down Ritual shared here is a simple practice to sustain your intention to live purposefully by planning your time and making space for what matters most to you. This process may support you in making powerful shifts, setting strong time boundaries, and realizing when you are falling back into old habits of saying "yes" to others while saying "no" to yourself. It will help you feel prepared for the week ahead, with clarity on what to expect. This allows you the advanced opportunity to create space where it is needed, and simply know that you have a plan and are in control of what you say "yes" to, and what you make space for.

Materials/Supplies Needed:

Feel free to use whatever tools work best for you. Whether you prefer to see how you spend your time laid out in a particular paper planner, an online calendar, a spreadsheet, or whatever form you can think of —this ritual works. You can keep it simple, or decorate it with intentional word stickers, whatever moves you. The key is to simply create the space to be intentional and reflect on how you are using your time.

• A space to track your time: journal/notebook/planner/spreadsheet
• Something to write with: a pen, maybe colorful pens/markers, and stickers, or whatever makes this fun
• You may like to find an Accountability Partner to support the process

Time Needed to Complete the Ritual:

30 minutes every week

Optimal Time of Day to Perform Ritual:

Weekly Planning Sessions should be held anytime between Thursday afternoon and Sunday evening (if your week starts on a Monday). Adjust as needed for your schedule.

I like to do my session on Friday mornings because it helps me identify the key things I need to have prepared to be ready for the next week—following up with scheduled appointments, making adjustments, sending out reminders, or gathering materials.

Best Time of Year to Perform Ritual:

All year - Weekly

Description of Ritual

You only have 1,440 minutes in a day. How you choose to use that time can be more fulfilling when you pay attention to what you say "yes" to. If you are intentional with your time, you can have more freedom, less stress, and more room for what really matters. Just like you might track your spending when you are trying to adjust your finances, or your meals when you are trying to adjust your weight or health through nutrition, you will use this process to track, review, and adjust how you spend your time.

The Wind Down Method uses four simple steps to allow you the space to prioritize your time:

- Step 1: Create Your Compass
- Step 2: Review and Reflect
- Step 3: Sync Your Calendars
- Step 4: Make Space For You

The first step takes a little more time and is often done annually with quarterly or monthly check-ins to make any edits. The remaining three steps are completed weekly during a thirty-minute, focused, pre-week planning session.

Step 1: Create Your Compass

Create a list of the most important intentions you have for your life. You will use this as a reference and guide as you move through the Wind Down process.

How would you like to categorize your time?

Some categories might be:

• Work/Volunteer

• Key Projects

• Financial

• Entertainment/Media

• Recreation

• Health/Self-care

• Hobbies

• Relationships

• Or something else

What are your key objectives for each category you created? Make sure you are clear on what success looks like for each. You can do this by mapping out clear SMART goals.

I have never been able to write a SMART list first but always use it as a checklist for what I have written and edited to make sure it meets the SMART goal criteria.

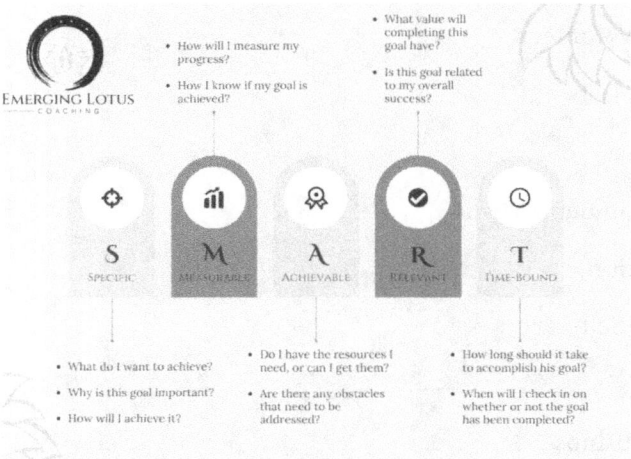

If you feel stuck, look back on how you spent your time during the past few weeks, and note what things excited and fueled you. What people, hobbies, etc. make you feel happy and support you in recovering from day-to-day stress? What people, activities, etc. depleted you and left you frustrated or stressed?

Now create SMART goals that support increasing the beneficial areas. For example:

• *Relationships:* Maintain a strong relationship with my adult daughter by texting at least weekly, and connecting personally, one-on-one, at least monthly.

• *Work:* Complete XYZ project by <month> and <date>.

• *Health:* Work out at least three times a week by doing yoga, lifting weights, and going for outdoor walks.

Step 2: Review and Reflect

Review how you spent your time over the past week:

• Compare your time to your weekly compass and rank your progress on your objectives. Did you move the needle forward on your objectives?

• Rank your time spent on each objective from 1-10 where 10 is you moved the needle the most ideal way possible for the week.

• Identify opportunities to refocus in the week(s) ahead for the lower rankings. Hold them for Step 4.

Make sure to celebrate your wins. You are making big changes with little steps by being intentional with your time.

Step 3: Sync Your Calendars

This step depends on your situation. Some people have only one calendar, and others have multiple calendars to reference. My family calendar can be referenced from my business calendar, but it doesn't automatically block off my time as "busy" if I am needed. In addition, I have several clients whose calendars cannot sync directly. I use this time to sync my time on my primary calendar to ensure I am not double-booked and that I allow time needed for travel or to buffer appointments.

This step is also great for people who like to have a digital calendar and a paper calendar. Ensure these are synced and account for all appointments and commitments to others. Or perhaps you can sync your project management tool with your calendar by assigning the time blocks needed to tackle the tasks for big projects

Here are a few things I recommend checking on as you sync your calendar:

• Make space between meetings. You can do this by scheduling one-hour meetings for fifty minutes instead, to create a buffer of five-to-ten minutes between schedules. There is nothing quite like not having enough time to go to the restroom, grab a drink, or breathe between meetings.

• Map out your travel time. It is easy to plug in your doctor's appointment, but not as simple to schedule enough time to get there, get back, and have a few minutes in between for the unexpected.

• Color code your activities by category to easily track them. This helps me easily note which activities are taking over, or slipping, at a glance.

Step 4: Make Space For You

Go back and make space for the items on your weekly compass. Pull forward the items you identified in Step 2 and schedule them. If the next week is already booked, what can you reschedule or move? If your week is locked in, with no room for adjustments, go to the following week and block off areas to protect your time. What gets scheduled gets done. Make sure you are touching the things that matter most. This is where you take your power back.

That is it! It only takes about thirty minutes a week to create this intentional space in your calendar and empower yourself to live the life you want, starting today.

Tips for success are:

• Schedule time in your calendar for your Wind Down pre-week planning—every week, any time from Thursday afternoon to Sunday morning.

• Having an accountability partner helps tremendously. Try connecting with a friend to help keep you accountable. If you are interested in a group, you can always check out our group here: https://www.emerginglotuscoaching.com/wind-down

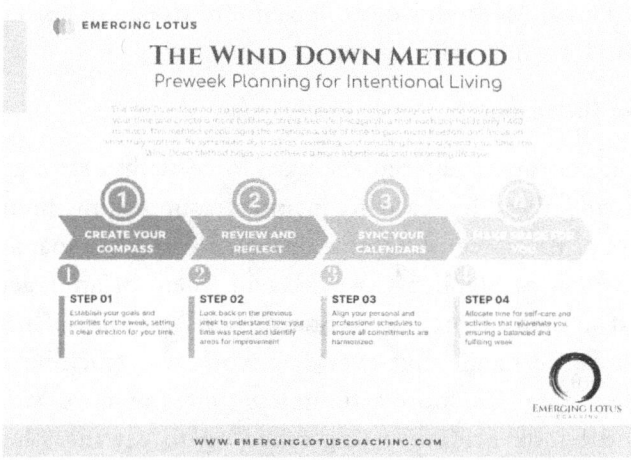

Share the Experience:

Living intentionally is to live with mindful awareness of the choices we make to fill our lives. You only have 1,440 minutes in a day. If you are not purposeful with your time, it may be stolen from you.

We live in an attention economy—where our attention is actually for sale. Software and tech designers are aware of our brain's rewards centers and how that impacts our behaviors, and they work to increase our connection with their products. This is not new. We have spent many years with businesses drawing us in via marketing because they understand how our minds work. This is why restaurants pump out a delicious smell to lure us in, why atmosphere matters at the grocery stores, and why shopping should be considered an Olympic sport for some Black Friday sales. We are lured in by the reward.

They are all jockeying for our attention, but we have the sole discretion of what we say "yes" to. The jobs we take, the food we eat, the people we surround ourselves with, what we watch, and so much more.

It is easy to lose time scrolling through social media, and then scrabble to manage the reduced time you have left. When we practice the Wind Down Method, we can have more freedom, less stress, and more room for what really matters.

Reflect on the Impact:

As a young mother, I entered the workforce with a strong desire to climb the ladder and increase my income to support my family. In the early years of my career, I became obsessed with time management. I read the works of Stephen Covey, David Allen, Brian Tracey, Laura Stack, and so many more. Laura Stack's *Leave the Office Earlier* held a magical promise to me, but even her work was teaching me to do more in less time. The more I did in less time, the more was assigned to me, and I took pride in being relied on to get the job done, no matter what. I was the "Yes person." The one who took on whatever challenge was handed to me, even if that meant going to work for twelve hours a day, or bringing it home to work on into the wee hours of the evening. Then a major clash of values at work significantly changed my process for time management—and the Wind Down Method was born.

My perspective began to crack when my young daughter proclaimed she would never follow in my professional footsteps because she "did not want to be overworked like that." Then, on a pivotal day, as I was leaving work to accompany my teenage daughter to receive the results of a crucial medical test, my boss asked me when I would return. I explained the gravity of the situation and informed her I was unlikely to return that day, emphasizing the importance of being present for my daughter regardless of the test outcome. My boss expressed discomfort with that decision and shared her feelings about the department's current staffing challenges and demands. She insisted I return to support the team. I refused, stating this was important enough that, if given the choice between my job and my daughter, my decision was clear; I would choose my daughter. Infuriated, I thought at first that my anger was directed at my boss. But with some reflection, I realized it was really directed towards myself. My time management had always been driven on "getting things done," and I had not held strong boundaries for my personal time and personal life. I had taught my boss to rely on me this heavily and that she could count on me to sacrifice anything for the needs of the job. So, I vowed to do better. I realized the real opportunity for change was how I managed my time and the boundaries I set around it.

Around this same time, I was introduced to Mindfulness, a practice that invites you to pay attention to the present moment and connect to yourself with openness and curiosity. I began a journey of living a more authentic life by being intentional about my choices—and that included how I spent my time. I remember clearly a time when I did not know what to do if I had an hour to myself. Now, I have a clear compass on how I want to spend my time, and I use the Wind Down Method as a practice to purposefully plan my time.

By following the four steps—creating my compass, reflecting on my past week, syncing my commitments, and creating intentional space for myself, I have been able to see easily when my commitments to others become off-kilter and make adjustments quickly. This process has helped me avoid burning out or straining my immune system with stress. It has made it easier for me to set boundaries around projects, be clear on my commitments, and ensure I am not just a hard worker, but also a committed mother, wife, daughter, sister, and friend. More than all that, I learned to hold the same integrity to my commitments to myself as I did to my commitments to others.

When I started to put limits on my availability, I was afraid it would be met with a negative view of my work ethic. Instead, people would ask me how I was able to be so aware and set strong boundaries. My leadership of my own time offered them permission to do the same. My clients have shared that this method has helped them shut down their computers and be present with family, friends, the outdoors, and themselves. It has helped them take up hobbies, and live a life of purpose and intention, rather than one where that is delayed for retirement. My favorite part of my own transformation is watching the reflection through my daughter as she navigates her profession being a hard worker who has boundaries and is living a full life.

Conclusion:

We are all in search of work-life balance. The reality is that *we* hold the key to the achievement of that. The biggest support in being intentional about your time is knowing what you want, and then making space for it. This can be challenging when you are programmed to serve the needs of others first but, by mastering the steps of the Wind Down Method, you can reclaim your time and focus on what truly matters. This process, which only takes thirty minutes between Thursday and Sunday each week, offers significant benefits: reduced stress, increased freedom, and aligning your values, so you feel truly empowered.

Living intentionally requires mindful awareness and deliberate choices. By embracing the art of mindful time management, you choose to fill your life with activities and people that uplift you and bring you joy. The Wind Down Method provides a practical framework to help you prioritize what truly matters. With the four simple steps of creating your compass, reviewing and reflecting, syncing your calendars, and creating space for yourself, you can build a life that aligns with your deepest values and aspirations.

Intentional living is not just about organizing your schedule; it's about reclaiming your power and creating an authentic guide amidst life's demands. This practice allows you to navigate your commitments with serene determination, while also ensuring time for self-care and quality moments with loved ones. By setting clear boundaries and making purposeful choices, you can break free from overcommitment and live a balanced, fulfilling life. Use the Wind Down Method to create a weekly habit of planning and reflection which will help you stay grounded, focused, and in control of your time. Embrace this opportunity to shine as the brilliant individual you are, and fill your life with joy and fulfillment.

**Follow the QR code to be guided through the Intentional Living:
Your Guide to Weekly Success**

About the Author

RACHEL CAREY-MCELWANEY

Rachel Carey-McElwaney, President of Emerging Lotus Coaching and Founder of the "Wind Down Method," is a passionate advocate for intentional living. With over twenty years of experience, Rachel helps individuals and organizations unlock their full potential and cultivate lives of purpose and fulfillment. Certified in HR, mindfulness, and coaching, she brings a unique blend of expertise to her practice.

Inspired by her journey as a young mother and corporate professional, Rachel developed the "Wind Down Method"—a revolutionary approach to intentional time management and pre-week planning. Her mission at Emerging Lotus is to empower individuals to discover their signature leadership voice, and nurture a culture of compassionate leadership, growth, and balance. As a contributing author to *Sacred Self: Rituals for the Modern Day Woman*, Rachel invites readers to embrace intentional living for transformative change in her chapter, "Beyond Balance: The Art of Living Intentionally."

Connect with Rachel at www.emerginglotuscoaching.com and @emerginglotuscoaching.

Writing With The Moon

FIVE YEARS AGO, I would never have believed it was possible to use the Lunar Cycles to help me write. At various stages throughout my life, I've spent a lot of time stuck in self-doubt as I battled the spectre of "Imposter Syndrome," and struggled with my self-worth as a woman and an author. On top of this, for years I suffered from an incredible fear of sharing my voice and, therefore, my work, with the world. But now, after learning to live by and work with the cycles of our beautiful Moon, I have developed a writing practice that helps me connect with my natural cycle and intuition to create a rhythmic sense of flow in my personal and business writing.

As writers (and creators), you can use the energies of the Moon to guide you to become aware of, and work through, any blocks that may arise from fear, self-doubt, lack of worth, or harsh inner judgement. You can learn when to set intentions, when to take inspired action, and when to rest. When to *be* and when to *do*. While I will give you an overview of the relationship between the Moon Cycles and writing, (and some suggestions about the rituals I have developed), it may take some time to figure out where your ease and flow lie in this process. Remember to be playful, have fun, and enjoy the experience.

The Ritual: Writing With The Phases Of The Moon

"Writing with the Moon" will help you create a simple ritual to tune into your emotions and open your creative channels.

NEW MOON

The beginning of the Lunar Cycle is a time of quiet, restful energy. The Moon is a sliver in the sky.

As such, it is the perfect time to:

• Tap into your creative mind

• Acknowledge and outline your writing goals

• Set your intentions and plan for the month ahead

• Be aware of fresh ideas that may appear in your consciousness through conversations, song lyrics, books, podcasts, media (social or otherwise), or your subconscious through dreams and signs from the Universe

Not yet in full creative mode, this is your opportunity to work with the beautiful energy of *being*, not *doing*. There is no need to act and "do all the things." Simply take care of yourself as you rest in awareness and create intentions and affirmations around the writing goals you desire to achieve.

WAXING CYCLE: Waxing Crescent Moon, First Quarter Moon, Waxing Gibbous Moon

As the Moon waxes, so does your creativity. Begin to *do*: follow your plan and take inspired action towards your intentions. You may find that your writing will flow more easily during the Waxing Cycle. Be patient, trust in the process, and know you are being fully supported by the energy and growing light of the Moon.

Waxing Crescent Moon

This is a time of delight and Inspiration. The week of the Waxing Crescent Moon is the time to start to work towards your intentions. Enjoy!

• Create a writing schedule and work with it!

• Develop a writing ritual that works for you; this may involve visualisation, meditation, even going for a walk before you write. (You will find some suggestions at the end of this chapter.) This ritual is up to you, so play around with what best enables you to tap into your creative energy.

After much trial and error, I found a quick ritual that works well for me. I simply sit at my desk, light a candle, take three deep grounding belly breaths to connect to Mother Earth, and imagine a white light streaming into my crown chakra as I connect with the Universe and visualise my writing goal. Then, as I feel myself open, I start to write.

Note: as an editor, as well as an author, I can't stress enough how important it is to not edit at this point. Write in a safe space of no judgement. Do not worry about spelling mistakes, grammar, or half-finished sentences. Get the thoughts out of your head and your heart and simply write!

First Quarter Moon

Here, at the halfway point, it's all about creating balance within your writing focus.

• Keep writing! But, as you continue to make progress, remember to give your body and mind time to rest.

• Keep your inspiration flowing. Step out into the world and observe what is around you. *I find it helpful to keep a notebook handy, or use the Notes app on my phone to jot down thoughts and ideas for the particular project I'm focussed on, or for future work.*

• Be aware of messages from the Universe—be open to receive.

Waxing Gibbous Moon

During this week, you may find that challenges arise. Doubt and tension are likely to creep into your consciousness; you may worry that you are not achieving your goal, your writing is not "good enough," or about what other people will think of your work. If this happens:

• Stop, assess, and rejig your goals if necessary

• Add other forms of creativity to help keep you focused

• Most importantly, keep writing!

This is also a great time to edit your work. Take a step back from being an "author," pop on your editor's hat, and use the energy from the Moon's growing light to illuminate your writing.

FULL MOON

The Full Moon is the perfect time to launch your book, share an important article, or release a new offer to your community. This phase serves as a time to "shine a light" on what you want to birth into the world.

The theme of the Full Moon is "release"—take the opportunity to acknowledge, then let go of, any attachment to the outcome. For writers, this relates to trusting in yourself and the energies of the Lunar Cycle, and believing that your words will be received by those who need to hear it the most.

As such, this is the time for completion. You may:

• Celebrate any intentions you have achieved

• Show appreciation and gratitude for all you have learned

• Be mindful and present as you finish editing and get ready to release your work to the world.

Shadow Work

I like to think of this as a time to be open to "shadow work"—seeing the depths within us while being supported by the light within and without. We are likely to experience heightened emotions during the Full Moon and when practicing Shadow work. Use them to drive your writing and try not to overthink.

WANING CYCLE: Waning Gibbous Moon, Last Quarter Moon, Dark/Balsamic Moon

The Waning Cycle is the time when we gradually move back into the space of "being" rather than "doing." Energetically, it's a great time to create awareness about your writing project by posting on social media, enjoying conversations, and sharing all you have learned during the process of creation.

Internally, the Waning Cycle is a time of reflection and growing awareness about what may be standing in the way of achieving the intentions you set during the New Moon.

Waning Gibbous Moon

You may find your writing is less "in flow" during this Moon phase, so this is a fabulous time to take a break! Do whatever makes you happy to nourish your body, mind, and soul:

• Rest

• Play music

• Enjoy a candle-lit bath

• Meditate

• Read

• Go for a walk /get out into nature

I often find that short, sharp bursts of writing work better during this phase, rather than sitting at my desk for hours. Adjust your ritual (and expectations) accordingly so you can harness this Lunar energy to its full potential.

Use this opportunity to continue to share your work, collaborate, create social media posts, speak on podcasts, or any other activities that are in tune with your intentions.

Last Quarter Moon

This final balance point can often be quite challenging as the Lunar energy ebbs towards the next New Moon. The best way to tap into and use this energy is to:

• Reflect on your writing process. *What worked for you and what didn't? What can be tweaked? How can you make the upcoming month work more smoothly, or more in flow?*

• Reassess your intentions. *What needs to be released? What can be carried into the next cycle? Do you need to be more specific in setting your intentions or creating your affirmations?*

• Take responsibility for any mistakes. *What have you learned? What adjustments can you make? How have you grown in your knowledge of yourself when working with the Moon?*

Journalling is hugely important in the last week of the Waning Cycle. Use journal prompts, free write, mind-map, or doodle—and start to notice any inspiration that will kick off your next month's writing experience.

Balsamic/Dark Moon

The Dark Moon is my favourite phase of the Lunar Cycle—but it is also the time I find the most challenging. My emotions are always high, and I have a strong tendency to "feel all the feels." Where possible, my ritual is to block these days out of my work calendar and "go within," thus allowing the energy and emotion to flow through me in cleansing preparation for the upcoming New Moon.

During this time of deep reflection and healing, you may find it incredibly helpful to:

• Retreat

• Connect to Spirit, the Universe, and your Higher Self

• Write in your personal journal and take note of any inspiration that grows from these raw, unfiltered feelings

• Take note of where you are being guided to explore in your future research and writing

On a practical level, this is also the perfect time to clean and declutter your desk, writing space, and office so you can begin the new month with a fresh and clear outlook!

During my struggles with the varying machinations of Writer's Block, I have also found it incredibly helpful to listen to chakra-balancing frequency meditations that relate to the particular Lunar Cycle at the time. Easily found with a Google or two, these meditations help me to clear my mind, heart, and soul from the trappings of self-doubt and tap into the flow of Lunar energy, thus allowing me to open my creative channels – and write!

Our beautiful Moon is with us all the time, shining from above as she creates a constant play of darkness and light. It is fascinating to explore how closely our personal cycles mirror those of the moon. Our creativity flows with her and can easily be guided by her ever-changing light in the sky. All we have to do is look up!

Writing Rituals to Help You Tap into Your Creative Energy

Humans love rituals. They help us focus. They create comfort. And they also help us take off one hat (parent/partner/sibling/child/friend) so we can put on our writer's hat.

Some options you can consider and have fun with are:

Music: *Do you write better with or without music? What sort of music? Classical, rock, pop, your favourite artist, relaxing sounds, a balancing frequency?* Spotify has heaps of writing playlists you can try out.

Space and Time: *Do you prefer to write in a particular space? Inside or outside? At home or a cafe? When does your creativity flow freely?* Play with different options until you work out what's best for you.

Your Tools: *Are you inspired by writing in pen? Do you prefer your laptop? Does it help to have coloured pens, blank paper, or Post-it Notes?* Have fun!

Focus: *Light a candle to draw your focus and let your body and mind know you are about to begin writing.* This will also create a lovely scent in your writing space.

Centre Yourself: *Ground yourself in your favourite way to centre your energy, focus, and get your ideas flowing.*

Spiritual Support: *Draw an Oracle card for guidance and inspiration. Depending on your beliefs, ask for guidance from Spirit / Universe / Source / God.*

Meditation: *An intentional meditation can help to focus and clear your mind.*

Your Breath: *Simply taking three to five deep belly breaths can be helpful, especially if you are feeling overwhelmed.*

Self-Love: *Anything easy you can do to help you get in the right headspace can be beneficial—like a shower to wash away your day or a ten-minute walk on the beach.*

Private Space: *Even shutting your office or bedroom door is a simple ritual!*

There are so many different options to try when Writing with the Moon—so be creative, play, and have fun! Find what sparks your energy and fills you with joy.

Follow the QR code for the Journal With The Moon Journal Prompts & Interactive Experience

Writing Rituals to Help You Tap into your Creativity

Humans love rituals. They help us focus. They create comfort. And they also help us take off one hat (parent/partner/sibling/child/friend) so we can put on our writer's hat.

Some options you can consider and have fun with are:

Music - *Do you write better with or without music? What sort of music? Classical, rock, pop, your favourite artist, relaxing sounds, a balancing frequency? Spotify has heaps of writing playlists you can try out.*

Space and Time - *Do you prefer to write in a particular space? Inside or outside? At home or a cafe? And when does your creativity flow freely? Play with different options until you work out what's best for you.*

Your Tools - *Are you inspired by writing in pen? Do you prefer your laptop? Does it help to have coloured pens, blank paper, Post-it Notes? Have fun!*

Focus - *Light a candle to draw your focus and let your body and mind know you are about to begin writing. (Plus it'll create a lovely scent in your writing space.)*

Centre Yourself - *Ground yourself in your favourite way to centre your energy and focus and get your ideas flowing.*

Spiritual Support - *Draw an Oracle card for guidance and inspiration. Depending on your beliefs, ask for guidance from Spirit / Universe / Source / God.*

Meditation - *Can also help with focus and clearing your mind.*

Your Breath - *Simply taking three to five deep belly breaths can be helpful, especially if you are feeling overwhelmed*

Self-Love - *Anything easy you can do to help you get in the right headspace - like a shower to wash away your day or a ten-minute walk on the beach.*

Even shutting your office or bedroom door is a simple ritual!

There are so many different options to try – this is the perfect time to be creative, play, and have fun! Tap into what sparks your energy and fills you with joy.

linktr.ee/ruth_fae_writer

About the Author

RUTH FAR

Founder of Fae Blood Publications, Ruth Fae is an Intuitive Writing Coach and Editor, Author, and Youth Mentor. A believer in the timeless and magical art of storytelling, she guides aspiring and established authors to align with their authentic voice and safely and confidently release their stories to the world.

Through working with hundreds of authors, Ruth sees the transformation that occurs when people are truly seen and heard. A rebel at heart, she trusts that we can create change in the world through sharing our stories and speaking our truth.

Ruth is published in nine diverse collaborative books, writes on Medium, and loves to explore the many facets of writing, parenting, and spirituality on podcasts. Her chapter "Writing with the Moon" encourages writers to use the energies of the Lunar Cycles to work through writer's block, tune into their emotions, and open their creative channels.

Residing in Melbourne, Australia, Ruth Fae shares her 'Life of Love and Magic' with her partner, their seven children, and an adorably naughty puppy named Merlin.

Connect with Ruth: https://linktr.ee/ruth_fae_writer

Survive to Thrive

NURTURE YOUR TRUE ESSENCE AND CRAFT YOUR SACRED SELF RITUAL

TRANSFORM YOUR LIFE: The Message Your Eighteen-Year-Old Self Needs to Hear

If you could give your eighteen-year-old self a message that could positively impact your life, *what would it be?* Imagine it as one sentence, a magic spell that can change your life for the better, simply by shifting your perspective.

I've thought about this a lot, and took the time to create my personal sacred message: *Invest in self-love and self-care.* This realization dawned upon me after years of unconsciously neglecting myself, unwittingly abandoning my own needs while also fearing failure and rejection. Little did I know that this self-neglect seeped into every aspect of my life, and influenced my mindset, thoughts, feelings, behaviors, and even my perception of the world around me. Indirectly, it also influenced my relationships. Does this sound familiar to you?

Feeling unworthy and insecure, I allowed myself to be treated poorly in various situations and relationships, unaware of the toll it took on my self-esteem and well-being. In the process of seeking validation from others, I found myself trapped in a cycle of pleasing behaviors,

148

anxious to meet the expectations of others so I could feel the illusion of being worthy. I changed my colors to fit into their image. Physically, these triggers manifested in various forms, from tightness in my chest to racing thoughts that kept me awake at night. It took me over fifteen years to step by step create more awareness of the negative impact the high dose of stress had on my experiences, health, and relationships..

Rediscover Your True Colors: The Journey from Insecurity to Self - Awareness

We've all heard of the fight, flight, and freeze stress responses to trauma triggers. A lesser-known survival mechanism is the fawn response, where one feels an obsessive need to change their true self to fit into the supposedly accepted image of those around them in order to feel accepted by the group. This is chameleon behavior: instead of staying true to your own colors, you adapt and adjust to the colors that others demand of you.

What are your True Colors?

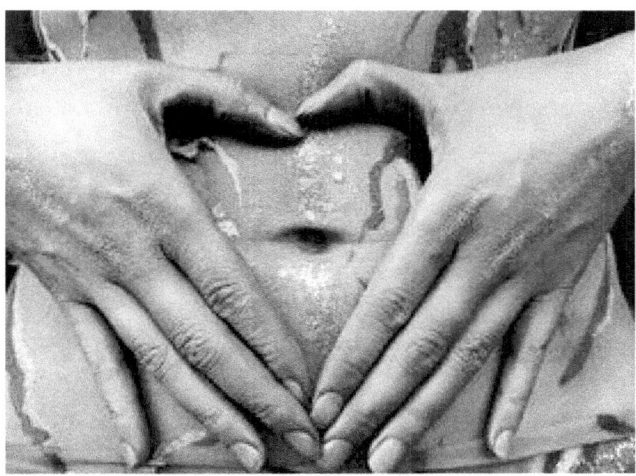

I invite you to empower yourself by discovering and crafting your sacred self-ritual. Below, I offer some examples and inspiration to get you started. Embrace your authentic self and remain faithful to your true colors.

It wasn't until I embarked on a transformative journey—loaded with nothing but a backpack and a yearning for something more—that I began to unravel the layers of neglect and rediscover my true essence. While traveling the globe for a year and a half, I found solace in the simplicity of life on the road. Amidst the vast landscapes and unfamiliar cultures, I discovered my inner sanctuary—a place of warm safety, a sense of home and inner-peace.

In this journey of self-discovery and empowerment, I learned the importance of navigating emotional triggers—the moments that threatened to pull me back into the depths of "survival mode." These triggers, whether they stem from past trauma or present stressors, have the power to hijack our emotions and send us spiraling into a state of chaos and fear.

Added to this, I discovered that we hold the power to shift from survival to thriving; it begins with intentional rituals. These rituals, carefully crafted to address our unique needs and desires, serve as beacons of light in moments of darkness. Through mindfulness meditation, conscious breathing, and sensory grounding techniques, we can anchor ourselves in the present moment, transcend the grip of our triggers, and reclaim our sense of peace.

One Percent for Wellness & Prevention: Small Actions, Big Impact

Prevention is key to maintaining a state of thriving. Self-care practices that nourish our body, mind, and soul are the first step. By embracing the one percent rule—taking the smallest action to improve your comfort by at least one percent, such as adjusting your pillow, reading one page, or journaling one sentence—and taking small, incremental steps towards our well-being, we can gradually build resilience and strengthen ourselves against future triggers.

Yet, despite our best efforts, we may still find ourselves succumbing to old habits of procrastination and avoidance. In these moments, it's essential to lean into rituals—such as journaling, goal-setting, and mindful self-reflection—that counteract self-sabotage. By cultivating a mindset of self-compassion and perseverance, we can overcome obstacles that stand in the way of our growth.

At the heart of it all lies the concept of the *Sacred Self*—a manifestation of our truest essence and deepest aspirations. As we craft personalized rituals that honor our identity and lifestyle, we strengthen our connection to our sacred inner sanctuary. It's a journey of trial and error, of small wins and gentle self-discovery, but with each step forward, we come closer to our ultimate flourishing.

So, to my eighteen-year-old self and all the women embarking on their journey of self-discovery, remember this: in the realm of modern womanhood, navigating emotional triggers isn't just about surviving —it's about thriving. Through intentional rituals and unwavering self-love, we have the power to transcend our limitations, embrace our true potential, and embody the essence of our Sacred Self. And remember, every small step forward is progress, every one percent counts towards our ultimate flourishing.

I'm curious now, what's your sacred message? Feel free to connect with me through the QR - code below and if you want you can share your sentence or sacred message— with me through e-mail or social media.

Craft Your Personal Sacred Self Ritual

To embark on a journey of self-discovery and empowerment, begin with the creation of your personal Sacred Self ritual—a sanctuary of self-care, mindfulness, and inner transformation. Imagine this ritual as a cozy haven, warmly inviting you to explore the depths of your being and embrace the richness of your inner landscape.

But how do you turn this vision into tangible action? The key lies in integrating practical behavioral management techniques into your daily routine, empowering you to take meaningful steps towards a life of greater fulfillment and balance. Picture waking up each morning with a sense of purpose and clarity, ready to infuse your day with intention and gratitude. This is the promise of crafting your Sacred Self ritual—a journey that is both inviting and achievable, guiding you towards a life that feels deeply authentic and satisfying.

In our exploration, we'll uncover the powerful connection between your lifestyle choices and your overall well-being, inviting you to make small adjustments that yield significant results. From nourishing your body with wholesome foods to cultivating a positive mindset through daily affirmations, each action you take is an opportunity to align with your true desires and values.

Join me as we embark on this adventure together, embracing the practical wisdom of behavioral management and the journey of shared experience. Together, let's create a space where you can learn, grow and shine your true essence upon your daily experiences with purpose and meaning. Get ready to step into your power, ignite your passion, and build the life you've always imagined—one intentional choice at a time.

1. Discover Your Inner Sanctuary and Nurture It with Self-Care

Crafting your personal Sacred Self ritual is a journey of self-discovery and empowerment that begins with the exploration of your inner sanctuary. This is a sacred space where you can connect deeply with your true essence and honor your unique needs and desires. Take a moment to reflect on activities and practices that bring you joy, peace, and a sense of fulfillment. Whether it's indulging in *creative expression* —such as journaling, painting, dancing, immersing yourself in nature, —or simply *savoring moments of solitude*, honor the unique essence of who you are and what resonates deeply with your spirit.

At the heart of your Sacred Self ritual lies the practice of self-care—a sacred act of nurturing your body, mind, and spirit. Embrace rituals that replenish your energy, uplift your mood, and cultivate a sense of inner peace. From indulging in luxurious baths and pampering skincare routines to practicing mindfulness meditation and journaling, prioritize self-care as a non-negotiable part of your daily routine. By honoring your needs with love and compassion, you create a foundation of resilience and well-being from which you can thrive.

Take the time to brainstorm and write down the activities you want to be included in your Sacred Self Ritual.

2. Awaken Your Senses with Mindful Practices

Elevate your Sacred Self ritual with mindful practices that awaken your senses and deepen your connection to the present moment. Practice activities that engage all six senses—sight, sound, touch, taste, smell and proprioception (awareness of how you position yourself in the world around you)—to cultivate a sense of presence and gratitude. Whether you savor a delicious meal mindfully, bask in the beauty of a sunset, or listen to soothing music with undivided attention, immerse yourself fully in the richness of each experience. By cultivating mindfulness in everyday moments, you awaken to the beauty and abundance that surrounds you, which fosters a deep sense of inner peace and fulfillment.

Choose an activity that engages all your senses: smell, taste, touch, sound, sight and proprioception. Observe your body during this activity; you might find it helpful to use the bodyscan meditation. This practice shifts your focus from the external to the internal, increasing your self-awareness and consciousness of your body and inner state. It helps you connect with yourself, create inner peace, and gain clarity and alignment, so you can better understand your needs and what actions to take. By collecting data on your experiences, you can track your progress from a survival state to a thriving state.

3. Embrace Rituals of Connection and Community

As you cultivate your Sacred Self ritual, recognize the power of connection and community rituals to nurture your well-being and foster meaningful relationships. Share your journey with loved ones, engage in acts of kindness and compassion, and seek out opportunities to connect authentically with others. Whether you gather with friends for a nourishing meal, volunteer in your community, or participate in group meditation sessions, cultivate rituals that foster a sense of belonging and connection. Nourishing your relationships and contributing to the well-being of others will create a ripple effect of positivity and love that uplifts you, and those around you.

4. Practical Tips to Navigate "Triggers": Shift your Mindset from Surviving to Thriving

Mindful Awareness and Mindset: Start by cultivating mindful awareness of your triggers. Take note of the thoughts, emotions, and bodily sensations that arise in response to triggering stimuli. For instance, if criticism triggers feelings of defensiveness or anxiety, observe how these reactions manifest in your body—perhaps as tension in your shoulders or a racing heartbeat.

By acknowledging these patterns, you gain insight into their underlying causes and empower yourself to respond more effectively. Shifting from a "fixed" mindset, where you might believe criticism is a personal attack that must be defended against, to an "abundant" mindset allows for different perspectives. For example, you could see criticism as constructive feedback that presents an opportunity for growth and improvement.

Practice cultivating this mindset through activities such as a *guided body scan or walk meditation*. During a body scan, you systematically focus on each part of your body, noticing sensations without judgment. This practice enhances awareness of how your body responds to stress and helps develop a more compassionate self-view. Similarly, walk meditation encourages mindfulness while moving, fostering a sense of calm and clarity that supports positive mindset shifts.

Breathwork: Harness the power of breathwork to calm your nervous system and induce relaxation. Practice belly breathing—inhaling deeply through the nose, allowing the abdomen to expand, and exhaling slowly through the mouth. In moments of turmoil, this simple yet potent technique can help alleviate stress and restore equilibrium.

Grounding Techniques: Grounding techniques are invaluable allies in times of distress. Engage your senses by focusing on the present moment—feel the texture of an object in your hand, listen to the sounds around you, or savor the taste of a soothing beverage. By anchoring yourself in the here and now, you diminish the grip of triggering stimuli and reclaim a sense of control. Another effective method involves tactile stimulation on your body: tap parts of your body, gently shake your limbs, or brush your skin. These actions can help bring you back to the present and alleviate distress.

Self-Compassion: Cultivate self-compassion as a cornerstone of your healing journey. Be gentle with yourself in moments of vulnerability, and acknowledge that triggers are a natural part of the human experience. Treat yourself with the same kindness and understanding that you would offer to a cherished friend who is facing similar challenges

5. Trial and Error: Embrace the process of change

Embrace the process of trial, error, and change as you navigate your personal Sacred Self ritual. As you experiment with different activities and rituals, allow yourself the freedom to explore and discover what truly speaks to your heart. Remember that there are no right or wrong answers—only opportunities for growth and self-discovery.

6. Celebrate Your Victories: 1% beats 0%!

If you begin to feel overwhelmed by the enormity of your goals, or by life in general, remind yourself that progress is not about achieving everything at once—it's about taking small, meaningful steps forward. As Dr. Glenn Patrick Doyle says, "Can't clean the whole room? Clean a corner of it. Can't do all the dishes? Do a dish. Can't take a shower? Wash your face."

Even in the face of daunting challenges, there's always something you can do with the energy and focus you have, if you want too.

Embrace the power of the one percent! When obstacles seem insurmountable in your journey towards crafting your Sacred Self ritual, break them down into manageable tasks and focus on making incremental progress. Each small victory, no matter how seemingly insignificant, is a testament to your resilience and determination. Remember, **1% beats 0% every time.**

Celebrate these victories as stepping stones on your path to transformation, knowing that every effort brings you closer to the life you envision.

7. Practice Makes Progress

Consistency is key to cultivating a meaningful Sacred Self ritual. Every day, set aside dedicated time to engage in practices that nurture your well-being and uplift your spirit. Whether it's a morning meditation, an evening gratitude practice, or a midday walk in nature, prioritize self-care as an essential part of your daily routine.

Ready to enhance your well-being?

Whether you're juggling home and work or simply seeking moments to recharge, our personalized coaching and corporate wellness consultations offer a supportive path forward.

In life's journey, finding harmony between responsibilities and personal sanctuary can be challenging.

Rituals serve as anchors, weaving together different aspects or dimensions of life to provide stability and connection with ourselves and others.

Our approach integrates personalized coaching, stress relaxation techniques, and corporate wellness strategies to support this integration. It's a space where the demands of professional life align with the need for personal growth and inner peace.

Are you ready to level up in different aspects of your life and take the next step?

Is your answer a 'yes'? Feel free to join us in navigating these challenges with authenticity and resilience. Start reclaiming balance and harmony today. Let's embark on this journey together, enriching every aspect of your life with purpose and fostering lasting well-being.

Scan the QR code to explore inspiration on crafting your own sacred self-ritual and learn more about how to connect with me for support in your healing and empowering journey. I'm looking forward to connecting with you!

Pura Vida, Charlotte

About the Author

CHARLOTTE DE JAEGHER

Charlotte De Jaegher, founder of Arasari Lifestyle, is a multifaceted wellness expert who blends the energy of her inner child with the wisdom of a global leader. With a background in physical education, corporate wellness, and coaching, she empowers individuals and businesses to overcome challenges and embrace positive transformation.

Through tailored sessions and workshops, Charlotte fosters well-being and productivity by drawing on her expertise in personal development, leadership, and stress management. As a bestselling author and experienced instructor, she shares her wisdom and warmth with others, inspiring them to lead fulfilling lives.

Charlotte's approach reflects the playful energy of the Arasari bird, embodying both curiosity and insight. Her vibrant spirit and dedication to holistic living inspire others on their journey to empowerment.

Contact details?
www.instagram.com/arasari.lifestyle/
www.facebook.com/ArasariLifestyle
www.arasari-lifestyle.com
arasari.lifestyle@gmail.com
charlotte@arasari-lifestyle.com

Nature Rest and Reset

❧

A SIT-SPOT PRACTICE TO REALIGN WITH YOUR INNER SELF AND TUNE INTO NATURE'S WISDOM

WHAT TO EXPECT:

This ritual helps you to slow down to nature's pace, and calms the distractions and mental chatter so you can return to your inner nature and tune in to listen to nature's wisdom. Stress melts away, your heart opens up to the natural world, and you gain a sense of groundedness, peace and clarity so you are better able to be present, and resilient in life's challenges.

Materials needed:

• Wear comfortable, appropriate clothing. If the weather is nice, I recommend taking your shoes off when you get to your sit-spot, and walking barefoot for extra grounding connection.

• Bring extra layers, a warm hat or sunhat.

• A hot beverage or water is optional.

• Optional: a folding stool or mat if desired.

What NOT to bring: Leave behind your to-do lists, notepad, or phone (or turn it off).

Time to complete:

Start with ten minutes and increase up to twenty minutes or more as you get more comfortable. When you sit for twenty minutes, you mimic the behavior of animals returning to their natural behaviors following a disturbance.

Optimal time to perform:

I find that I like this activity when there's less activity at the nature sit-spot location. But you can do this at any time of the day or evening all year-round.

Description of ritual:

Purpose: Nature is always speaking to us, but are we attuned to hear? Often, we are too busy rushing around from place to place to listen. We tend to move through our lives mindlessly and rapidly, so the natural world goes unnoticed.

Rachel Carson said it beautifully:

> *"For most of us, knowledge of our world comes largely through sight, yet we look about with such unseeing eyes that we are partially blind. One way to open your eyes to unnoticed beauty is to ask yourself, 'What if I had never seen this before? What if I knew I would never see it again?"*

~Rachel Carson, The Sense of Wonder

In our modern world, we move constantly—striving, competing, amassing, overworking—devoid of play and joyful moments of non-doing. Yet if we slow our pace in nature, be mindful of our actions and thoughts, value moments of play and non-doing, and focus our attention to nature, we experience profound benefits to the mind, body, and spirit.

You are not only a part of nature, you *are* nature, a part of its multi-colored fabric. Every breath you take is exchanged with the plants and trees. The food, clothing and shelter come from the same atoms that make everything on the planet. You are part of the cycles of birth, living, and death in various forms.

By tuning into the rhythms and seasons of nature, you can learn how nature recycles, regenerates, transforms, and has periods of hibernation and growth spurts. In fact, nature cannot survive, or fails to thrive, if it doesn't go through its inherent cycles of activity and inactivity.

When you don't slow down and intentionally connect with the natural world, you lose touch with nature as well as your inner nature. You are inextricably intertwined and interdependent with all of Nature.

Nature has been around for much much longer than humans, and there is great wisdom in the trees, birds, and sky for those who tune into the language of nature through intentional attention.

This ritual is designed to help you open your awareness and slow down your mind chatter so you can reconnect with nature for rest and replenishment. Time in nature brings you into a mindful awareness of the world around you; you quiet the analytical mind so you can listen with your heart. To see beyond what is physically there, to be in stillness to hear nature's wisdom.

Trees, birds, the wind, are all messengers, but are you open to receiving this wisdom?

Basically you will sit for ten or more minutes and notice with all your senses. Start with five-to-ten minutes and work up to at least twenty minutes, at which time they will return to their normal movements and behaviors and you're more likely to see them. This is a mindful activity that brings you to present moment awareness.

Choosing your sit spot

Choose a location in your nearby nature where you can sit for about twenty minutes. This place doesn't have to be a grand botanical garden, state park, or wild nature location. It's best if it is nearby, a place you can get to easily, like a spot in your yard, local park, or nature space.

Alternative: If you cannot go outside, you can sit by a window that looks out to nature, and open the window a bit so you can smell and hear.

Ritual:

Pre-ritual: This practice begins when you embark on your walk to your sit spot. Walk with intention to your sit spot, acclimating to nature's pace, notice your breath and the speed at which you are walking.

If you are walking quickly, slow down and perhaps take a breath with every other step..Breathe in, step left foot, breathe out, step right foot, In, Left, Out, Right, repeat. You'll be matching the speed at which nature is moving.

Open your awareness with your senses: Notice the colors, textures and shapes as you walk.

When you arrive at your sit spot location and sit down, notice what is by your feet and above you.

Sensory Awareness

Begin with Vision: Vision is our dominant sense and we have the ability to see so much, yet we tune out most of it. With our eyes, we perceive such things as color and texture, size and shape, movements and distance.

What do you see around you? Notice the *trees or plants.*

• How many are there?

• Are they dense or sparse in distribution?

• Are there flowers or seeds or fruit?

• Is there any *movement* from the wind or animals?

• What *colors*—how many shades of green or brown?

• Do you see texture like stripes, wrinkles, smooth, bumpy?

Listen for Nature's Symphony: I prefer to close my eyes for this part because it helps focus my attention to listening. You can choose to keep your eyes open or closed, depending on your situation.

Listen for the loudest sound, and then for the quietest sound.

• What directions are the sounds coming from?

• How far away? Are they beside you or in the distance?

• Are there sounds that bother you? Or that you find pleasant?

Sense of Smell:

What does the air smell like?

• Do you see something for which you can conjure up the smell from memory?

• Is the air fresh, warm, stuffy?

• Is there a smell that is spicy or floral or orange-blossom-like?

Sense of Touch: From our scalp down to our toes, we have the ability to discern textures and temperature with our skin.

• How does the air feel on your skin?

• Or the clothing touching your body?

• What does the surface feel like beneath your seat or feet?

• How do you feel temperature-wise? Chilly or comfortable?

If your mind chatter is particularly annoying, come back and focus on your senses. Take a breath and notice how it feels, what's beneath your feet, or the sounds you hear. Remind yourself you will have plenty of time to get to that "To-do" list later!

Notice what catches your attention; a swaying branch or the call of a crow...

As you sit and take in your surroundings, take mental note of what you see. Let your mind be in wonder and awe. What makes you curious? How does it make you feel?

Afterward: This is optional, but you might like to journal what you noticed—in nature or about yourself.

• Did something stand out to you?

• Did it bring you to a state of wonder and curiosity?

• What did you feel like before and what did you feel like afterward?

The more you write about your thoughts and emotions, the more you increase your emotional vocabulary and emotional intelligence.

Some things to be aware of

As you sit, you may go through several states of being. The following states may not necessarily be in order, but know that when you observe your thoughts and feelings, and let it be seen and felt, they will pass.

• **Excitement:** To try something new that will bring peace and connection, and is the pathway to replenishment.

• **Discomfort:** Of not "doing" anything, of possibly "wasting time." This time is not wasted: ten minutes spent sitting in nature saves you more than ten minutes in increased clarity, creativity, calmness, and productivity, as well as being in a better mood so everyone around you benefits too!

• **Fear of missing out (FOMO):** Or rather, the fear of missing something that might be important: "I need to remember to call Mary," or "I need to stop at the store on the way home," or "I need to write this down," or "take that photo." When we release ourselves from the grip of FOMO, in trust that it's all ok if we don't do "everything," and begin to come back to our senses (sight, smell, hearing, taste, touch), then we return home to our inner selves.

• **Boredom:** The state of being bored feels like nothing inspires you, nothing is catching your interest, everything feels flat and "the same" —homogenous. This ritual is not a time of idleness, but can stimulate creativity and new ideas. The mind chatter quiets and makes space so you can receive insight.

• **Insight:** New ideas can emerge from time spent in non-doing. Instead of being focused on an activity, let your mind and body relax so your inner wisdom can rise to become surface awareness. When our minds are not occupied with analytical thinking, we can open our awareness to the world around us in the present moment, and nature can facilitate the emergence of new ideas. You might find solutions to a particular question drop into your awareness.

Personal Experience:

One of my favorite mindful connective practices is nature journaling —being in nature and recording my conversations with nature with drawings, words, and color in a sketchbook.

But sometimes, I need something more to bring me back to a grounded center.

During my nature journaling, I noticed that I was losing my quiet connection to nature, and was simply "going through the motions" on a page. Then a voice inside me pointed out that I had forgotten to journal something I saw the previous week, and the other day on my walk, and the cool eagle I saw two days ago... and I felt that I was recording the experience unconsciously instead of enjoying it.

I felt a desire to spend time *just sitting* with the garden plants, or listening to the birds, without constantly having to identify and record my "data." Nature journaling was supposed to be fun and separate from the accurate data collection in my science work. But much of the time, it was hard to settle into the "feeling" heart space I desired.

I realized I needed to temper that analytical part of my mind that kept urging me to continue "doing" and did not allow me to stop to rest.

Although nature journaling is a nourishing practice that brings me joy, peace, and connection, if done unconsciously it can become another task I need to do. Over time, it can become a to-do list item instead of the replenishing time it is designed to be.

While you might not have participated in nature journaling, there may be another activity or behavior you enjoy—but part of you is pushing in a way that takes the joy out of it.

I do this ritual when I find myself feeling overwhelmed, uninspired, or irritable! These feelings are a sign that I've lost connection with my inner, or higher, self. This practice helps me to reconnect and re-align with nature's higher wisdom, and regain mental and emotional clarity, creativity, calmness and joy.

By sharing what happened recently when I did this ritual, I hope to make you aware of the potential of similar resistance or roadblocks arising for you.

One morning, my mind chatter was particularly loud, barking orders about all the tasks I needed to be doing, *now!* So I knew I needed to get outside and do one of my go-to calming and grounding rituals. And I felt that *this time it needed to be different,* without any note-taking, journaling or technology. It had to be just me and Nature—without barriers or distractions.

So, on a sunny morning, around ten o'clock, I pulled out a camping chair and sat outside my front steps in the walkway to the garden. At first *I was excited, anticipating* what I might encounter while listening to the morning birds, and relaxing to see and be with the plants in my garden.

Within a couple minutes *I got fidgety* and it was hard to sit still. I kept thinking of the things I needed to do instead of focusing on the experience in front of me.

Then the fidgeting turned to *discomfort of "not doing."* I recognized that I have an unconscious reaction to jump up and DO when I'm in a quiet space—but there have been times where I could relax into it. This time, I hadn't been focussed on rest for quite some time, and my well was dry.

My next thought was, "Oh I need to sketch the flowers that are blooming now and the birds that I'm hearing so I don't forget." This was followed by, "I need to be connecting to nature with my nature journal." But at this time, I would have done these things on the surface level, not in a deeply meaningful way.

Sitting with the discomfort of not responding to the fear of missing something or *FOMO*, eventually turned to *boredom*. "Now what? What am I doing here? When will I be done?"

My mind was like a distracted puppy that just wanted to play and couldn't sit still. After a few moments of just *being still* through my changing emotions, I *received insight*—the insight that I had been aware, watching my thoughts as they manically raced through various emotional stages. This insight, the answer to a problem I had been trying to solve, simply dropped into my awareness.

When I can be quiet and still in nature, and focus on my senses, the chatter clears so I can hear the message that is meant for me. The wisdom that nature was trying to convey to me. In stillness, I receive clarity and guidance.

Ultimately, my advice to you is to physically still yourself, then mentally still yourself so you can hear the insights and messages meant for you. Make time to sit with nature, and return to this place as often as you can. And even if you cannot physically go to your sit-spot, you can close your eyes and visit in your mind's eye. See the space, the trees or grass, hear the birds, and smell the air. You'll begin to cultivate a personal connection over time that brings replenishment, renewal and insight.

About the Author

MELINDA NAKAGAWA, M.SC

Melinda Nakagawa, M.Sc, is an internationally recognized naturalist and nature connection mentor who has led workshops at Stanford University, Monterey Bay Aquarium, local museums and educational institutions, and has featured on various podcasts. She founded Spark in Nature to develop offerings that bridge science, nature, art, and heart to awaken one's innate connection to nature, and stimulate an intuitive ability to listen creatively to the language of nature.

She uses various tools, such nature journaling—a practice that brings a deeper nature awareness and connection through sketching to see, and writing to understand, the natural world in an open-hearted, playful manner. She's inspired hundreds of people to successfully move beyond their fears to draw with ease, and retrain their sight to see beyond ordinary nature to reveal unseen wonder. Melinda shares her unique process to move from not noticing nature, to living with intentional awareness, peace, joy, and wonder.

Join Melinda for her nature journal travel trips and workshops or become a member of Spark Collective, an online learning collaborative for nature journalers and creative entrepreneurs to connect, inspire, and expand their work.

Website: SparkinNature.com

Instagram: @sparkinnature
Facebook: Sparkinnature

Sanctuary of Sensuality: The Environment Ritual

CREATING SPACES THAT IGNITE PASSION

WHAT TO EXPECT **from the Ritual/Practice:**

Embark on a transformative journey to enhance your environmental awareness—a crucial component of your sexual wellness. The Environment Ritual emphasizes the importance of harmonizing your physical surroundings to revive your sexual vitality and deepen your connection to your sensual self. Through this focused practice, you are invited to carefully modify your environment to reflect and support your sexual desires and overall well-being.

As you engage in this singular ritual, expect to forge a profound relationship with your surroundings, and create a space that inspires, ensures safety, and reflects your deepest desires. The process involves selecting elements that evoke a sense of tranquility and allure, such as calming colors, inspiring artwork, and sensory details like specific scents or textures that resonate with your aesthetic and sensual preferences.

This journey encourages you to reconnect with the pleasure and power inherent in your intimate environment. By transforming your space, anticipate a reawakening of dormant passions and a heightened appreciation for the settings that frame your daily life. This ritual is not just about aesthetic changes; it's about embracing a transformative approach to how you inhabit and perceive your personal spaces. The benefits of this dedicated practice are far-reaching—expect enhanced emotional clarity, increased sexual pleasure, and a renewed vigor for life.

This experience celebrates self-love and empowerment, and guides you to a more integrated and vibrant expression of your sexuality. Each step of the Environment Ritual is a deliberate act of self-care that sets the stage for sustained sexual wellness and more profound personal satisfaction.

Materials/Supplies Needed:

1. Candles: Choose candles that resonate with you, perhaps scented with essential oils like jasmine or sandalwood which are known for their arousing properties and ability to enhance mood.

2. Journal and Pen: Bring a pen and a journal or notebook for reflecting on and recording insights that may arise during the ritual.

3. Comfortable Seating: Arrange a comfortable place to sit, such as a cushion, chair, or meditation pillow, where you can remain undisturbed for the duration of the practice.

4. Soft Fabrics: Gather soft, comfortable fabrics to create a nurturing space. These could be blankets, scarves, or a yoga mat.

5. Music: Prepare a playlist of music that inspires and relaxes you, and will aid in the creation of a supportive atmosphere for deep emotional and sensual exploration.

6. Essential Oils or Incense: Select essential oils or incense sticks that stimulate or calm the senses. Lavender, rose, or ylang-ylang are excellent choices for promoting relaxation and sensuality.

7. Crystals: If you use them, choose crystals like rose quartz for love and healing, amethyst for clarity and protection, or black tourmaline for grounding.

8. Natural Elements: Consider including fresh flowers or a bowl of water to enhance your connection to nature and the sensory experience.

9. Personal Artifacts: Any personal items that hold significant emotional or spiritual value, as they can help anchor your intentions and enhance the ritual's significance.

Time Needed to Complete the Ritual:

To fully immerse yourself in the transformative experience of this ritual and reap its benefits, set aside *48 to 72 hours* to create and refine your space. This extended period is an exciting opportunity to arrange your environment thoughtfully, and incorporate elements that enhance tranquility and personal resonance. Use this time to gradually introduce changes and adjustments, ensuring that each addition deeply aligns with your intentions and contributes to a harmonious atmosphere.

Optimal Time of Day to Perform Ritual:

Early morning or late afternoon is the best time to perform this ritual. Typically, these periods offer tranquility and fewer distractions, which allows you to focus intensely on arranging and harmonizing your space. Morning hours can harness the fresh energy of a new day, while late afternoon provides a transition into a peaceful evening, and sets a serene tone for relaxation.

Best Time of Year to Perform Ritual:

Timing is essential for this transformative ritual, particularly when you're navigating significant changes in your romantic life.

Whether a relationship has ended, you're seeking new love, or you're experiencing stagnancy in your current relationship, performing this ritual can be a powerful act of personal alignment and renewal.

Conduct this ritual during these pivotal moments to help you reflect on your desires, process your emotions, and set clear intentions for your future romantic endeavors.

You will take proactive steps toward healing and growth by engaging in this practice when you need emotional clarity or a fresh start. This approach ensures that the ritual is a meaningful and effective tool to support your journey through the complexities of love and relationships.

Description of Ritual

The Environment Ritual, a cornerstone of the SHE-BE-ME™ transformative experience, focuses on cultivating sexual wellness and personal empowerment for women. This unique ritual explores the profound interplay between our surroundings and sense of self, and emphasizes the importance of harmonizing our external spaces to enhance our overall well-being and sexual vitality.

Environment Ritual:

This exclusive aspect of the SHE-BE-ME™ experience is dedicated entirely to you. It involves creating a uniquely-you space that reflects and supports your sexual and holistic well-being.

The process includes tailoring your immediate surroundings to enhance relaxation, inspire sensuality, and foster a deep connection with your personal and intimate desires. Through the thoughtful placement of meaningful elements such as candles, artwork, and natural features, you will transform your environment into a sanctuary that resonates deeply with your essence, and enhances your spiritual and emotional comfort.

This ritual is fundamental to a broader journey towards self-discovery and empowerment. By aligning your living space with your deeper needs, the Environment Ritual ensures a harmonious balance between your external environment and your internal state, to support a revitalized and sexually fulfilling existence. This focused approach allows you to reconnect with your passions and reclaim a sense of empowerment in your personal space and life.

The SHE-BE-ME Holistic Framework of a Woman's Sexual Desire™

Women are complex beings with multifaceted lives. Their sexual desire is influenced by a multitude of factors, not just one single element. Recognizing this complexity, I developed the SHE-BE-ME™ framework to address the diverse needs of my clients:

SPIRITUAL: Spirituality enhances sexual wellness by deepening connections with oneself and partners, and aligning sexual practices with personal values for enriched intimacy and authenticity.

HEALTH: Health, including physical and mental well-being, is fundamental to sexual wellness. Managing chronic conditions and stress is crucial for maintaining a fulfilling sex life.

ENVIRONMENT: Sexual wellness is influenced by the environment. A safe and supportive setting boosts libido and overall health, while awareness of environmental pollutants helps protect the hormonal balance.

BODY: Understanding and caring for the body enhances sexual satisfaction and health. Regular check-ups and awareness of the media's influence on body image are vital.

ENERGY: Energy, as a dynamic aura around all beings, interacts with our emotional and physical states. Sexual connections are enhanced through practices like meditation and energy healing.

MIND: The mind shapes sexual desire and identity. A healthy mental state fosters clear communication and robust emotional connections in intimate relationships.

EMOTIONS: Emotions are crucial in shaping the dynamics of intimate encounters. Enhancing communication and empathy leads to more fulfilling and consensual sexual experiences.

As you engage in the Environment Ritual, it's essential to personalize the experience to suit your unique preferences and needs. This will enhance the ritual's effectiveness and deepen its impact.

• Incorporate personal symbols that resonate with you—objects connected to significant life milestones, your cultural heritage, or spiritual beliefs—to enrich the emotional and spiritual dimensions of the practice.

• Select music and scents that evoke the desired emotions and ambiance.

• Adjust the timing of the rituals to moments when you feel most alert and receptive. To ensure they become a nurturing and sustainable part of your routine, tailor the duration and frequency of the rituals to fit seamlessly into your daily life.

• Set clear personal intentions to focus your activities, whether you're seeking to enhance relationship dynamics, foster self-love, or heal from past emotional wounds.

• Feel free to adapt the activities—such as replacing journaling with painting or another creative expression—to better align with your expressive preferences.

• Finally, decide whether these rituals are more beneficial for you as private sessions or should be shared with a partner or supportive community.

By trusting your instincts and customizing these aspects, you will ensure these rituals are powerful tools for transformation and rejuvenation.

Environment Ritual: Harmonious Haven

Purpose: Optimize environmental factors to support sexual desire and health.

Reorganize Your Bedroom

Employing Feng Shui principles can enhance relaxation and intimacy by creating a harmonious environment. Here's a guide to rearranging your bedroom to promote love and positive energy:

Declutter and Simplify

• **Remove Clutter from the Bedroom**: Excess items create stagnation and disrupt the flow of energy (Chi).

• **Items to Keep:** Keep only essentials and items that bring joy or have sentimental value. This allows for a stronger energy flow and reduces distractions, setting the stage for a calm, welcoming space.

• **Clothing:** If you have not worn something for over a year, toss or donate it.

Arrange the Bed for Balance

• **Position the Bed for Command:** Place the bed in a "command" position, meaning you can see the door from the bed without being directly in line with it. This placement offers a sense of security and control.

• **Headboard Stability:** Ensure your bed has a solid headboard, symbolizing relationship stability and support.

• **Equal Access:** Ensure equal access to both sides of the bed, representing balance and equality in a partnership. Each side should have its nightstand, creating a sense of harmony and fairness.

Choose Soft Colors and Textures

• **Warm and Neutral Tones:** Opt for soft pinks, earthy beiges, and calming blues, which evoke warmth and serenity. These colors, associated with the Feng Shui Bagua area of Relationships, enhance romantic energy.

• **Comfortable Textiles:** Use soft fabrics for bedding, curtains, and rugs. Textures like silk, velvet, or plush cotton create a sense of luxury and sensuality.

Incorporate Symbolic Elements

• **Pairs and Symmetry:** Include pair items to symbolize balance and partnership. This can be as simple as two matching lamps, artwork, or decorative objects.

• **Art for Love:** Choose artwork that depicts harmonious relationships or natural beauty. Avoid images that evoke loneliness or conflict.

• **Mirrors with Care:** If you have mirrors in the bedroom, ensure they're not facing the bed directly, as this can disrupt sleep and intimacy. Mirrors should reflect light and energy without interfering with rest.

Introduce Nature and Light

• **Plants for Fresh Energy:** Add indoor plants like peace lilies and orchids, which are believed to bring fresh energy and symbolize growth and renewal. Avoid plants with sharp or spiky leaves, as they can create tension. If you have pets, make sure the plants are pet-friendly.

• **Natural Light and Soft Lighting:** Allow as much natural light into the bedroom as possible, and use soft, warm lighting for evening hours. Lighting should create a cozy, romantic ambiance.

Embrace Personal Symbols and Intentions

• **Intentional Decorations:** Choose decorations that align with your intentions for the space. This could be crystals, personal mementos, or spiritual symbols representing love and connection.

• **Set Intentions for the Space:** As you rearrange the bedroom, set intentions for relaxation and intimacy. You can vocalize or write these intentions, focusing on creating a supportive and loving environment.

By following these Feng Shui-inspired steps, you can create a bedroom that fosters relaxation and intimacy; a harmonious setting for love and deeper connections.

Sensory Enhancement

Sensory enhancement in a bedroom is about creating a multi-dimensional experience that appeals to and calms the senses. You can transform a bedroom into a haven of relaxation and intimacy by thoughtfully introducing elements that engage touch, smell, and sound. Here's how you can expand on sensory enhancement:

Touch: Soft Fabrics and Textures

• **Plush Bedding:** Choose high-quality bedding made of soft, breathable fabrics like Egyptian cotton, bamboo, or silk. These materials provide a luxurious touch that encourages comfort and relaxation.

• **Layered Textiles:** Introduce layers with quilts, throws, or blankets made from soft materials like cashmere, fleece, or velvet. This adds warmth and coziness to the space.

• **Cushions and Rugs:** Scatter decorative cushions on the bed and place a plush rug beside it. These tactile elements enhance comfort when lounging or getting in and out of bed.

• **Furniture Selection:** Choose furniture with inviting textures. Upholstered headboards or soft, curved chairs can be a soothing addition, encouraging relaxation.

Smell: Essential Oils and Aromatherapy

• **Essential Oils:** Diffuse essential oils like lavender, chamomile, or sandalwood to create a calming atmosphere. These scents are known for their soothing and stress-relieving properties.

• **Incense and Candles:** Burning incense or scented candles with subtle fragrances can enhance the olfactory experience. Opt for scents that promote relaxation and intimacy, such as ylang-ylang, jasmine, or patchouli.

• **Potpourri and Fresh Flowers:** Display potpourri or fresh flowers in the room for a natural and inviting aroma. Flowers like roses and tulips not only add beauty but also impart a pleasant fragrance.

Sound: Calming or Sensual Music

• **Background Music:** Play calming or sensual music to set the mood. Soft instrumental tracks, smooth jazz, or classical music can create a tranquil ambiance, while soft romantic melodies enhance intimacy.

• **White Noise:** If you prefer a quieter environment, consider using a white noise machine or a fan to drown out external sounds and create a serene atmosphere.

• **Soundscapes:** Experiment with natural soundscapes, such as gentle rain, ocean waves, or forest ambiance. These natural sounds can be soothing and help facilitate relaxation and sleep.

• **Acoustic Design:** If possible, improve the room's acoustics with soft furnishings, such as curtains and rugs, to reduce echo and create a more inviting sound environment.

Sight and Light

• **Soft Lighting:** Use dimmable or adjustable lighting to create a warm and inviting glow. This flexibility allows you to adjust the light to suit different moods.

• **Decorative Accents:** Add visually pleasing decorative items like art, photographs, or objects that reflect a soothing or romantic theme. These elements engage the visual sense and contribute to the overall atmosphere.

After completing your ritual, take a moment to reflect on your experiences and insights. Open your journal and write down any thoughts, emotions, or realizations that surfaced during the practice. This reflection helps you internalize the impact of the ritual, track your progress, and identify areas for further exploration. Journaling—a powerful tool for self-discovery—allows you to capture the subtle shifts in your journey and record your personal growth. Don't rush; let your thoughts flow freely without judgment or censorship.

Share the Experience:

When embarking on this transformative journey, I immersed myself in the ritual to explore and understand its impact. I committed to refining my environment, a crucial aspect of the SHE-BE-ME™ experience, with a mix of hope and caution. I focused on creating a sacred space that mirrored my innermost desires, by incorporating sacred stones and meaningful objects that rekindled my connection to my core. This spiritual process allowed me to sense the divine energy and embrace new beginnings.

As I delved deeper into the ritual and discovered its profound transformative power, I restructured my living space to promote relaxation and sensuality, dispel stagnant energy, and infuse a vibrant, nurturing ambiance. This physical and energetic cleansing brought a profound sense of peace and grounding, which led to significant shifts in my mental and emotional clarity. By the end of the ritual, I felt a deep connection with myself, and a renewed zest for life. The experience was about more than just enhancing sexual energy—it was a profound journey of self-reclamation.

Reflect on the Impact:

This transformative ritual allowed me to shed layers of doubt and self-neglect, and reconnected me with a more intuitive and authentic self. It illuminated the role of the environment in nurturing well-being and sexual vitality by showing how a harmonious space can profoundly influence one's spirit and emotions. At the end of my journey, I felt empowered and complete, with each element of the environment contributing to a renewed sense of self. This experience has had enduring effects; it fostered patience, openness to intimacy, and courage to explore desires. It was a powerful testament to the resilience of the feminine soul and the potential of embracing one's whole self.

Conclusion:

Feeling sexually and spiritually alive is essential to a woman's overall well-being. The Environment Ritual, focused solely on creating a harmonious living space, provides a targeted approach to rediscovering and nurturing this vital aspect of life. This ritual empowers women to take control of their surroundings and, by extension, their emotional and sexual health.

It's a powerful tool for anyone seeking to enhance their quality of life, promote self-acceptance, and celebrate their inner beauty. As such, this ritual is more than a practice—it is a gateway to a more fulfilled and empowered existence, and reminds us that the journey toward sexual wellness is profound and essential.

About the Author

ALLIE THEISS

Allie Theiss, a distinguished sexologist and sex and integrative wellness coach, is the visionary behind the SHE-BE-ME female sexual desire model. A board-certified sexologist with a rich background in psychology and integrative wellness, her expertise shines in her work, particularly her ritual for connecting to female sexual desire.

Beyond her academic and professional achievements, Allie created "Out of Body Ecstasy," which offers unique "anytime, anywhere" orgasmic experiences. Featured in Cosmopolitan and Playboy, her creative and playful spirit is further showcased by her passionate screenwriting career and love of collecting vintage jewelry.

Visit Allie at ThePassionZone.com and embark on a journey of sexual empowerment by signing up for her enlightening newsletter, bridging the gap between sexual wellness and overall health.

Connect with Allie:

- https://www.linkedin.com/in/allietheiss/
- https://www.facebook.com/thepassionzone
- https://www.instagram.com/passionzonestore/

About the Publisher

Inspired Hearts
Publishing

Inspired Hearts Publishing is passionate about sharing inspiring stories of men and women who've overcome great hardships, experienced untraditional success, and are carving out their own path in life —stories of hope, inspiration, strength, resilience, love, and transformation.
We thrive on providing a platform for business owners to leverage their personal story, experience, and expertise to grow their audience and establish themselves as an expert in their industry.
If you loved this book, please give us a 5 star review on Amazon or GoodReads
and
Send us an email at write@inspiredheartspublishing.com

Inspired Hearts Publishing is passionate about sharing inspiring stories of men and women who've overcome great hardships, experienced untraditional success, and are carving out their own path in life —stories of hope, inspiration, strength, resilience, love, and transformation.

We thrive on providing a platform for business owners to leverage their personal story, experience, and expertise to grow their audience and establish themselves as an expert in their industry.

If you loved this book, please give us a 5 star review on Amazon or GoodReads
and
Send us an email at write@inspiredheartspublishing.com.

FIND us at www.inspiredheartspublishing.com

SCAN ME